Social Engagement
& the Steps to Being Social

*A Practical Guide for Teaching
Social Skills to Individuals with
Autism Spectrum Disorder*

Kathleen Mo Taylor, OTR/L
Marci Laurel, MA, CCC–SLP

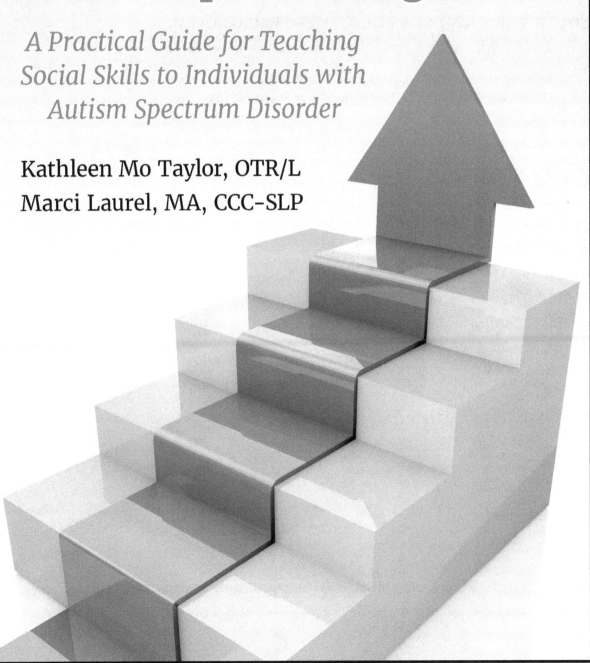

SOCIAL ENGAGEMENT & THE STEPS TO BEING SOCIAL:

A Practical Guide for Teaching Social Skills to Individuals with Autism Spectrum Disorder

All marketing and publishing rights guaranteed to and reserved by:

FUTURE HORIZONS INC.

721 W. Abram Street
Arlington, TX 76013
(800) 489-0727
(817) 277-0727
(817) 277-2270 (fax)
E-mail: *info@fhautism.com*
www.fhautism.com

© 2016 Kathleen Taylor, OTR/L & Marci Laurel, MA, CCC-SLP

Cover & interior design by John Yacio III

To acquire pages available for copying, access http:/fhautism.com/socialengagement.html.

ISBN: 9781941765104

Contents

Contents

Foreword

Social skills are essential to life success. In school, good social skills boost academic performance; increase students' interest in learning; improves learner behavior; prevents and reduces bullying; and improves school climate (cf. Civic Enterprises et al, nd). At work, social skills are essential to employment success with recent trends revealing that requirements for social competence in the workplace have increased dramatically. Moreover, employment and wage growth is strongest in jobs that require high levels of both cognitive and social skills (cf., Deming, 2015).

Despite the recognition that social skills contribute heavily to life success, few curricula have focused on the skills that are foundational for social skills acquisition. Even fewer have addressed the needs of individuals across the spectrum—from a classic presentation to those with average-to-above average intelligence.

This wonderful book fills this void. It begins with instructional strategies for the most basic social skills; self-regulation, shared space with a skilled partner, shared pleasure, and shared focus. It then moves to strategies that address skills that range from proximity to growing connections. The book is (a) solid, (b) evidenced-based, (c) focused on the research in social engagement, (d) practical, and (e) easy to read and implement. *Social Engagement & the Steps to Being Social* is one of those rare books that can benefit the reader who is new to social skills instruction and the user who is a veteran instructor.

This book should be in every classroom and every job development site. It should be available to parents who foster the social development of their child and it should also be accessible to individuals on the spectrum so that they understand the complexity of engagement and social skills. I cannot recommend this book enough.

When asked to write the foreword for *Social Engagement & the Steps to Being Social*, I planned to read rapidly through it to gain an impression. However, I found the content so intriguing that I slowed my reading to ensure that I learned the information presented here and even read the book a second time. I know that you will do the same!

—*Brenda Smith Myles, Ph.D.*
The Ziggurat Group

References

Agran, M., Hughes, C., Thoma, C. A., & Scott, L. A. (2014). Employment social skills: What skills are really valued? *Career Development and Transition for Exceptional Individuals, 39*(2), 111-120.

Civic Enterprises, Peter D. Hart Research Associates, Bridgeland, J., Bruce, M., & Hariharan, A. (nd). *The Missing Piece: A National Teacher Survey on How Social and Emotional Learning Can Empower Children and Transform Schools. A Report for CASEL*. Washington, DC; Collaborative for Academic, Social, and Emotional Learning.

Deming, D. J. (2015). *The growing importance of social skills in the labor market* (No. w21473). National Bureau of Economic Research.

Introduction

We began working together in 1987, providing occupational and speech-language therapy co-treatments for children who had sensory processing and communication struggles, including those with autism. As young therapists, we worked very hard to address the needs of the many amazing children we worked with and learned from week to week. Over time, however, we understood that there was something we had not studied in school or even thought much about that was an important link to success for so many. We realized that we needed to learn how to teach children not only motor and communication skills, but also how to use those skills in relationships with other people.

Over the past 25 years, we have been on a journey to discover, describe, and teach "social skills." The model presented in this book has had many incarnations, from checklists to diagrams; we even conceived it as a picture frame one especially creative year! As we began conceptualizing the steps, we learned that each step should be broken down into still others, allowing for the opportunity to analyze "being social" and support those for whom it does not come naturally. As you will see, the "steps" are more of an escalator, ever moving and influenced by much that happens within the day-to-day interactions of a real person's life.

Before we begin, we offer a few comments to help navigate the content. First, words associated with the model and used to communicate the specific definitions provided therein are in boldface, italicized, and capitalized. These include *FOUNDATION, ENGAGEMENT, READY, LOWER 4, MIDDLE 4,* and *UPPER 4*. The book is divided into four areas representing the skill sets of the model: *FOUNDATION, LOWER, MIDDLE,* and *UPPER 4*. Within each area is a description of the skills encompassed there, along with vignettes describing the social world of one individual with Autism Spectrum Disorder (ASD). At the end of each section, skills are broken down into smaller sub-steps. Evidence-based practices (EBPs) to support the skills in each area are then described, followed by a case study. After *FOUNDATION*, you will find a description of general strategies that support *ENGAGEMENT*. At the end of *LOWER, MIDDLE,* and *UPPER 4*, one sample intervention objective and activity to match each step is provided. Note that these are included as a framework for developing activities for intervention and meant to spark your own creativity as you support the development of social skills at each step across people and settings in a variety of ways.

It is our hope that people who have an interest in promoting social skills – family members, teachers, therapists, and the individuals they care about so deeply—will find *Social Engagement & the Steps to Being Social* to be a meaningful and practical guide. Our goal is to address both a growing understanding of the nature of what it means to be in social relationships with others and how to "step on" to the learning process on any given day and over time. Indeed, as we have learned from many extraordinary teachers, the process can be exhilarating!

Why Are Social Skills So Important?

Have you ever had time with a friend that you have not seen in years and been amazed by the experience of picking up just where you left off? Natural conversation highlights the magic of reciprocal social interaction that is both self-sustaining and mutually satisfying. The ease of these moments can mask the dynamic interplay of the subtle yet complex skills required.

Social skills are the skills we use to communicate our messages, thoughts, and feelings and to interact with each other (http://dictionary.reference.com/). These skills are the context for all learning, a prerequisite for positive adult outcomes and a deeply important part of being a person. Furthermore, impairments in social communication that are part of the diagnostic criteria for ASD include social-emotional reciprocity, nonverbal communication behaviors, and developing, maintaining, and understanding relationships (American Psychiatric Association, 2013). Those of us working with individuals with ASD must continue to develop our abilities to assess and teach these critical skills.

How did you learn the complex understanding we define as social skills? When you walk into a restaurant, office cubicle, movie theater, or public restroom, how do you know how close to be to another person, when you should or should not make eye contact, how much you can talk, or what is the appropriate tone of voice or topic of conversation? Indeed, it is a wonder that we ever know how to be! However, we act "intuitively," based on years of observation and corrective feedback that might have been very direct, especially when we were children, or quite subtle as we note another person's response to our own behavior. For individuals with ASD, and others who struggle to develop social skills, these skills need to be well assessed and taught directly. Think about something that is hard for you to do, maybe writing or spelling, packing the car, or reading a map. While others may find these tasks natural and proceed without thought, you have to understand your own area of weakness and develop strategies to compensate for a lack of skill. We all have areas in which we need to work harder than other people to succeed at something that is important to us. Remembering this can help us empathize with the incredibly hard work it is for many individuals with ASD to operate in a social world.

For all of us, and especially school-age children, learning happens through social experiences that are defined by unwritten rules and an expectation that certain ways of being together are inherently understood (Endow, 2012; Winner, 2007). For example, even very young students in a classroom are expected to stay together and make transitions as a group. They need to understand that they are "one of many"; that is, when a direction is given to the group they are expected to follow it and, conversely, they cannot interact with the teacher as if there is no one else in the room (Gray, 2000). In addition, key areas of academic development require social understanding. Consider, for example, that the ability to comprehend a story necessitates discernment of character relationships and motivations as well as the ability to infer and predict social behavior. Clearly, social skills, which allow us to share space and experience with other people, are not just for making friends. We need our social skills to function well in everyday life (Winner, 2005).

Social skills are also paramount in considering outcomes for adults with ASD. Difficulties with social communication have been cited as roadblocks for adults with ASD in both higher education and places of employment (Barnhill, 2007; Thierfeld Brown, Wolf, Kind, & Bork, 2012; Tincani & Bondy, 2015; Endow, Mayfield, & Myles, 2012). Clearly, the development of academic skills, while obviously important, does not ensure success for individuals with ASD in post-secondary school settings or in the workplace. Rather, social skills (such as the ability to maintain calm, exchange important pieces of information, understand a common goal, be flexible and collaborative, understand hierarchy, and consistently follow the myriad of social rules that govern behavior) are essential (Myles, 2016). Undoubtedly, any director of human resources, working with people with or without disabilities, would say the same.

Equally important to the development of appropriate school and workplace skills is the ability to develop satisfying personal relationships that enrich each person's quality of life. In the past, we have sometimes made the mistake of misinterpreting a lack of social skill as a lack of interest when trying to understand the lives of individuals with ASD. What we now understand is that everyone, including those who struggle to learn social skills, desires connection with other people and seeks comfort, safety, and a sense of belonging as part of a social community.

A strong premise for this model is that social skills and related strategies must be taught directly and with deep respect to individuals with ASD. Consequently, the development of these skills will not be supported by simply having the person who is struggling with "being social" spend time with others who have well-developed social skills. The analogy of teaching reading to a person with dyslexia is instructive; one would not seat a struggling reader with a group of strong readers and expect significant or meaningful improvement in the struggling reader's skills. Rather, assessment must inform instruction, and each pre-requisite skill must be taught in a structured manner before that skill can be integrated for use. The same holds true for teaching social skills to individuals with ASD.

As we plan for direct teaching of these essential skills, we consider who will provide this instruction as a social communication partner. Initially, we learn to be engaged with a *skilled partner (SP)*, often a family member or professional who has high motivation for interaction and proficiency with the skills being learned. We see that as we move up the steps to being social, *trained peers (TPs)*, who are a similar age to the learner and are taught skills to facilitate specific aspects of "being social," are key. Like the skilled partner, the trained peer is also motivated to be a part of the social interaction and has already mastered the skills he or she is helping to teach. In addition, while trained peers understand their role as teacher, they are also a true participant in age-appropriate activities and need frequent encouragement to understand their role in the success of the learner. Over time, learners increase their competence and confidence to use skills with the people they encounter in their day-to-day lives.

Finally, it is crucial to understand that all communication is social. While children may learn to talk or use alternative forms of communication, these have little value if social skills are not developed to provide opportunities to use communication for meaningful interaction (Frea & Vittimberga, 1999; W.D. Frea, personal communication, December 3, 2015). In fact, in the most recent revision of the *Diagnostic and Statistical Manual of Mental Disorders* (*DSM-5*), social and communication impairments were combined into one domain reflecting that social skills are inextricably linked to the development of communication skills (American Psychiatric Association, 2013; Schreibman et al., 2015). As you will see in the next chapter, ***ENGAGEMENT***, which we define as that remarkable ability to be self-regulated and share space, focus, and pleasure with another person, is where we begin our journey to "being social."

CHAPTER

1

ENGAGEMENT as the FOUNDATION

What does it mean to be "engaged" with another person? No matter what age or level of social development, certain key components define the moments that we are actively involved in connection with someone else. Consider an infant who uses her limited motor skills to signal that she is ready to begin or end a face-to-face interaction. Or the toddler who throws food off the high chair tray with delight at watching an adult pick it up, only to begin the game again. These are the early moments of **ENGAGEMENT** that become the foundation of a lifetime of "being social." Current research is helping us understand that very young children who are later diagnosed with ASD show a marked lack of orientation to the faces of their important people, while at the same time a heightened orientation to objects. This difference creates a change in early relationships as caregivers find a little one who does not respond to them in the ways that they expect; in turn, this often results in fewer opportunities to engage in and practice social interaction (Rogers & Dawson, 2010; Fuhrmeister, Lozott, & Stapel-Wax, 2015; Klin, 2014).

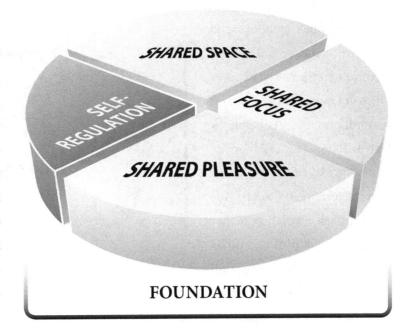

Self-regulation and shared space, focus, and pleasure are defined as the components of **ENGAGMENT**. The interactions designed to support **ENGAGEMENT** are usually facilitated by a skilled partner, often a family member in collaboration with a teacher or therapist. Similar-age peers can also be highly motivating and provide models for targeted behavior at this stage of learning. We will see that peers can be taught to directly teach targeted skills. For us, development of the **FOUNDATION**, born of a desire to understand the essence of what it means to be "engaged" with another person, has been one of the most enlightening aspects of this work.

Annie will help you get to know "ENGAGEMENT" ...

At four-years-old, Annie is most soothed when sitting straight backed, legs extended out while rocking forward and backward in a rhythmical pattern. Annie was diagnosed with ASD at 18 months. She has no verbal communication and uses simple gestures and vocalizations to get her needs met. She loves cylindrical items such as straws, hoses, tubes, and pipes. She enjoys being outside, playing in water, and looking at shiny silver items. Her parents work hard to find items of interest and play that keep her in "their world."

ENGAGEMENT

Self-Regulation: Calm + Alert = READY

Everyone can think of a time when they have not been "ready" to engage in social interaction. Perhaps you had a hard day at work and just want to close the door in a quiet room. Maybe you are worried about a loved one and therefore not able to focus on other people in your life or just feel overwhelmed. Self-regulation can be considered the ability to gain control of one's emotions and body to maintain and sustain attention for the task at hand, at all stages of our lives (Shonkoff & Phillips, 2000; Gillespie & Seibel, 2006). This task may be school work, running a business, or just "being social." We think of self-regulation as being in an emotional and physical place to learn and respond positively to each situation. One needs to be able to be calm and at the same time alert enough to focus on another person and share experiences together (Kalberg, Laurel & Taylor, 2013; Williams & Shellenberger, 1996).

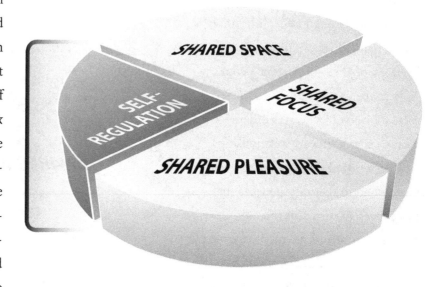

A key tenet of this model is that without self-regulation, there can be no ***ENGAGEMENT*** and without ***ENGAGEMENT*** there is no climbing the "social steps." It becomes crucial then to understand the signs that an individual is ***READY*** and to have ideas about how to help him or her get ready for ***ENGAGEMENT***, both at the beginning stages of learning and at any other moment of dysregulation.

Annie is self-regulated and ***READY*** to engage for about half of her pre-school day. At home, Annie has more options to help her regulate and less need to be on a specific schedule; therefore, she is regulated a bit more of the time. When regulated, Annie looks toward people with interest yet often does not make eye contact. Her body is calm and she appears to be aware of where she is and how she is moving through space. At these moments, Annie is in control of her emotions, not too frustrated, mad or sad, and not too happy. She might be making noises and moving rhythmically; this appears to help her maintain her regulated state. This is what self-regulation looks like for Annie and when she is in her best place to engage.

It is helpful to consider what types of sensory input (tactile/touch, auditory/sound, visual/sight, olfactory/smell, gustatory/taste, vestibular/movement, proprioception/position) can support an individual's self-regulation and what type of input can help a person remain regulated throughout a social interaction (Laurel & Williams, 2014; Williams & Shellenberger, 1996). Ayres (1979) stated, "When the whole body and all of the senses work together as a whole, adaption and learning are easy for the brain" (p. 37). More than 30 years later, discussing young children with ASD, Tomchek, Little, and Dunn (2015) stated, "Children's sensory processing patterns affect a child's ability to sustain active engagement in activities that provide social communication opportunities" (p. 6). Clearly, being **READY** is critical to learning any skill, including "being social."

Questions to consider when trying to help an individual maintain self-regulation include:

- What type of sensory input is coming into a person's system in this particular social environment?
- Does there seem to be too much input or too little input?
- Is there a way to adapt or modify the type of input coming in?
- What type of sensory input is the person seeking?
- Does that sensory input support the person to be calm, alert, and **READY**?

***ONLY** when self-regulated can one begin to share space to pursue a positive social interaction.*

ENGAGEMENT

Shared Space: A Place to Be Together

This component of the **FOUNDATION** is defined as being in proximity to another person. As we grow and develop our social skills, we can "share space" over longer distances and even remotely, for exam-

ple, by phone or text. However, for the purposes of our discussion, it is critical that we begin by thinking about an individual's ability to be close to a communication partner, often within less than five feet. New learners need to be close enough to understand how to share focus and pleasure. Being aware of the space between ourselves and the person we are hoping to engage is extremely important (Richter & Oetter, 1990).

Guiding questions as you begin to think about places to share space include:

- In what settings is this person comfortable?
- What proximity to others does this person currently prefer?
- How can you visually define the space to help this person understand what is expected?
- How will you limit or organize materials within the space to encourage **ENGAGEMENT**?

Within a shared space, we can begin to be attentive together.

> When Annie is regulated, the space she is comfortable sharing is quite close, often within three feet. She seems to notice objects in her peripheral field, but she responds best to other people who seek **ENGAGEMENT** when they are visually in front of her. During facilitated social interactions, Annie needs three-dimensional boundaries, with the space visually defined using furniture, walls, or people's bodies. Success requires carefully timing the entrance and exit into and out of this space, which continues to be in the three- to five-foot radius. Limiting the materials of interest in this space and using materials with a definite purpose appear to support Annie to share the space, at moments when she is regulated, for more and more of her pre-school day and at home. Her skilled partner must share in Annie's space and then present a highly motivating item for shared focus to support **ENGAGEMENT**.

ENGAGEMENT

Shared Focus: A Reason to Be Together

Shared focus is defined simply as two people paying attention to the same thing at the same time. Initially, we work to understand the interests of individuals with ASD and to promote shared focus using items and activities that excite them as they do the hard work of being together. Perhaps you did not imagine engaging quite so much about dinosaurs, cars, or even coat hangers or plumbing! However, we understand how crucial it is to reinforce the beginning steps of sharing these interests with another person.

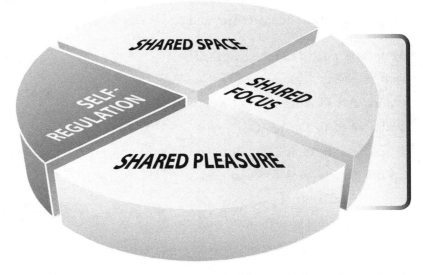

Guiding questions as you begin to share focus include:

- What is the person most interested in doing (e.g., objects, topics, movement)?
- Does the person try to bring your attention to something he or she likes and, if so, what action is taken to accomplish that?
- Are you able to bring the person's attention to something you select?
- How long can you share focus together?

Now that we are on the same topic, we can begin having fun together.

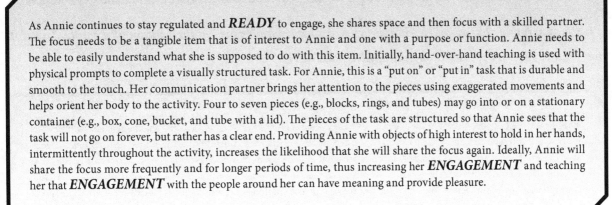

As Annie continues to stay regulated and ***READY*** to engage, she shares space and then focus with a skilled partner. The focus needs to be a tangible item that is of interest to Annie and one with a purpose or function. Annie needs to be able to easily understand what she is supposed to do with this item. Initially, hand-over-hand teaching is used with physical prompts to complete a visually structured task. For Annie, this is a "put on" or "put in" task that is durable and smooth to the touch. Her communication partner brings her attention to the pieces using exaggerated movements and helps orient her body to the activity. Four to seven pieces (e.g., blocks, rings, and tubes) may go into or on a stationary container (e.g., box, cone, bucket, and tube with a lid). The pieces of the task are structured so that Annie sees that the task will not go on forever, but rather has a clear end. Providing Annie with objects of high interest to hold in her hands, intermittently throughout the activity, increases the likelihood that she will share the focus again. Ideally, Annie will share the focus more frequently and for longer periods of time, thus increasing her ***ENGAGEMENT*** and teaching her that ***ENGAGEMENT*** with the people around her can have meaning and provide pleasure.

ENGAGEMENT

Shared Pleasure: Enjoying the Moment Together

Finally, the moment cannot be defined as **ENGAGEMENT** if there is no shared pleasure or enjoyment of the moment together. It is essential to be aware that each person shows pleasure in his own way, and for our learners with ASD, it can require careful observation to determine these cues. Prizant, Wetherby, Rubin, Laurent, and Rydell (2006) described social competence as "communication and playing with others in everyday activities and sharing joy and pleasure in social relationships" (p. 3).

We understand that cultures have their own languages, culture-specific behaviors, and social interaction styles. As described in the TEACCH model, teachers, therapists, and parents can function as "cross-cultural interpreters," translating the social world around our friends with ASD and, therefore, expanding their options for learning (Mesibov & Shea, 2011). This in turn expands our options for sharing true pleasure together.

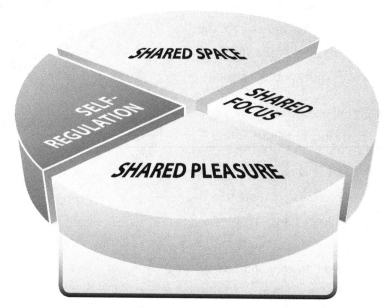

As you identify moments of pleasure for the people you work and live with, consider:

- What nonverbal cues are associated with enjoyment for this person?
- Who knows the person best and can help you to understand the person's unique cues?
- How and where can you observe the person to better understand how he or she shows happiness?

It is the synergy of shared space, shared focus, and shared pleasure in the context of a calm, alert state that defines the very special moments of ENGAGEMENT.

Shared pleasure can look different for everyone. Annie does not always laugh or smile when she is engaged. At times, her pleasure is expressed through a glance, a body gesture, or just an internal knowing that the skilled partner has connected with her. It can be brief or sustained. It looks different at pre-school than it does at home. Shared pleasure is a sense of being with another person. These moments of shared pleasure are what reinforce Annie to keep doing the very challenging work of "being social." We know the desire is there; the challenge is to teach her the skills for **ENGAGEMENT**.

Sub-Skills of ENGAGEMENT

We have seen that **ENGAGEMENT** is the foundation of all social development and we have considered the four components of **ENGAGEMENT**: self-regulation, shared space, shared focus, and shared pleasure. These early components of "being social" need to be broken down into even smaller, measureable, meaningful sub-skills. A sub-skill for our purposes is a measurable, critical mini-skill that when combined with others can lead to proficiency in one of the components of **ENGAGEMENT**.

Measuring a small skill which comes so intuitively to others is a challenge. In this model, we will rate the sub-skills of **ENGAGEMENT** using a concrete dichotomy: YES, the learner is observed to use the skill in a social situation, or NO, the learner does not use the skill in a social situation.

As you can imagine, individuals will have specific times, places, and people that best allow them to demonstrate the sub-skills of **ENGAGEMENT**. Furthermore, if an individual is unable to self-regulate, it is important to recognize that the circumstance is not a teachable social moment and that self-regulation needs to be addressed. In contrast, if a person is self-regulated but having difficulty sharing space, focus, or pleasure, it is important to work in this area to succeed in moving up the steps to being social. The goal is to acquire a YES on all the sub-skills to make moving into the **LOWER 4** more successful.

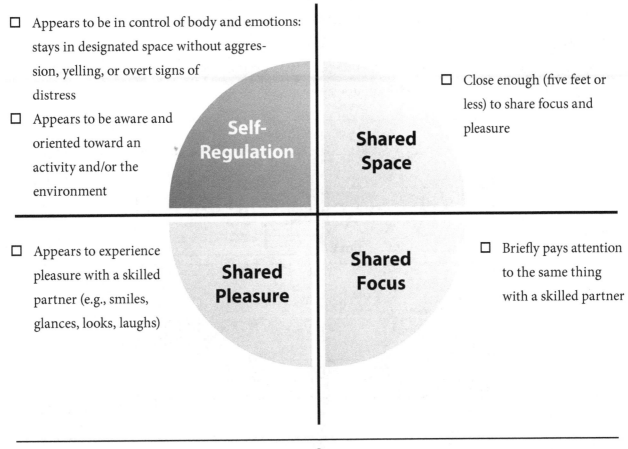

☐ Appears to be in control of body and emotions: stays in designated space without aggression, yelling, or overt signs of distress

☐ Appears to be aware and oriented toward an activity and/or the environment

Self-Regulation

Shared Space

☐ Close enough (five feet or less) to share focus and pleasure

☐ Appears to experience pleasure with a skilled partner (e.g., smiles, glances, looks, laughs)

Shared Pleasure

Shared Focus

☐ Briefly pays attention to the same thing with a skilled partner

Critical Strategies to Enhance ENGAGEMENT

Shrink the space

Arranging a setting or environment to create boundaries often helps the learner feel comfortable, focus on the task at hand, and understand that he is with a social partner. For example, you can move to a corner of a room instead of the middle, sit as opposed to stand, or bring peers in on each side of the learner and use their bodies to build a "container," a safe space, if you will, to help the learner realize we want him to share the space for a period of time.

Use motivating items or topics

Determining a person with ASD's items of interest is one key to success. This can be done by asking family members, observing in different environments, presenting items that provide various sensory input, and respecting that each person has items and ideas that spark interest. This process can take patience. Is the person's interest in the light rays moving in and out of his peripheral vision, is it a colored hanger and the way that it moves, is it the wind on his face when he runs, is it the car magazine, or the neighborhoods in Albuquerque, New Mexico? Is it the characters on *Star Trek* or the beat of certain music, or sink drains or *Minecraft*? Whatever it is, everyone has something that is motivating, and we need to find out what that is to support true social ***ENGAGEMENT*** (Grandin & Panek, 2014).

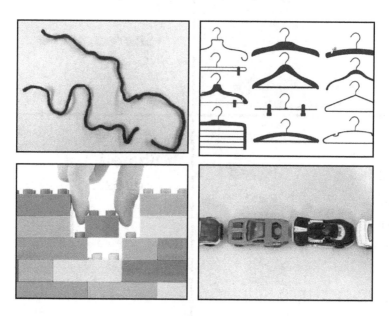

Limit the materials

The facilitator of the social interaction needs to be:

- In control of when a preferred item is available
- Able to make the preferred item available within the time span an individual is able to pay attention

In addition, it is critical to realize that more than one or two motivating items should be made available because an individual will become bored and satiate on only one motivating item or topic.

Increase the duration and frequency of the engaged moments

When you find those moments of **ENGAGEMENT**, you should work to hold them for a longer period of time. Look for opportunities to make them happen more frequently. These moments need to be practiced in a variety of settings, with a variety of people, and using a variety of items.

Identify and teach others the importance of ENGAGEMENT

Everyone needs to understand that being **READY** and then sharing space, focus, and pleasure is the foundation to understanding the social world.

Evidence-Based Practices (EBPs) to Support ENGAGEMENT

Evidence-based practice is a process for informed decision making. In this process, results of high-quality research are used in combination with professional expertise and individual and family preferences to determine appropriate practices to use for a specific intervention. This process makes clear that the experiences, values, and preferences of educators, interventionists, and those with whom we work should contribute equally to our clinical decisions. As with all interventions, ongoing assessment and data collection are critical to ensure that the interventions are effective for a specific individual (Boehm, 2016). Also, remember that our work in intervention is a blend of art and science; each professional, along with the family members with whom she partners, will bring her own history, personal skill set, and creativity to the amazing job of teaching social skills.

The National Professional Development Center (NPDC) on ASD is one source of information for learning about and using evidence-based practices, including information briefs, steps for implementation, and fidelity checklists (http://autismpdc.fpg.unc.edu/). The NPDC website provides links to Autism Focused Intervention Resources and Modules (AFIRM), with modules for learning about evidence-based practices. In addition, the National Autism Center has identified established and emerging treatments through the National Standards Project (www.nationalautismcenter.org). Many practices are identified by both organizations. Evidence-based practices linked to Social Engagement & the Steps to Being Social are based on practices defined by the NPDC.

Information about evidence-based practices in autism is available to practitioners and parents. These practices cover an enormous range of skills and abilities. Practically speaking, it is especially important to learn to use knowledge about ASD, understanding of a specific individual, and clinical judgment to match the right practice with a specific goal for learning. Too often, a well-researched practice is used to support the development of a specific skill for which it does not make sense. Consider how the wrong screwdriver, even a brand new and well-crafted one, can derail afternoon plans for a simple home project. Similarly, employing well-known, useful practices such as social narratives, social groups, and video modeling, when applied at the early stages of *ENGAGEMENT*, is often ineffective.

The following EBPs have been shown to support aspects of *ENGAGEMENT* and have proven effective in our own practice to teach the *FOUNDATION* of "being social."

- **Task analysis** is "the process of breaking down a skill into smaller, more manageable steps in order to teach the skill" (Franzone, 2009 p. 1). Task analysis has been used to address academic, behavior, communication, and social skills—any skill that can be broken down into smaller steps. Indeed, this entire model is a task analysis of what it takes to "be social" and right at the beginning it is important to break down each social challenge into its component parts. What smaller skills will allow an individual to be calm and alert and then share space, focus, and pleasure?

- **Reinforcement** "describes a relationship between learner behavior and a consequence that follows the behavior" (Neitzel, 2009, p. 1). As many of you well know, positive reinforcement, giving something that increases the chance that a specific behavior will happen again, is used in many aspects of teaching. When working to bring individuals with ASD into a circle of **ENGAGEMENT**, and indeed for all the steps to "being social," it can be especially important to remember that we might need to make our reinforcement more tangible and provide it with greater frequency. When social interaction is such hard work, just being together with another person is often not enough to support the person to perform the extraordinary labor of social interaction. Identifying potential "reinforcers," such as highly desired objects and topics, and replenishing them with new ones as needed, is essential.

- **Prompting** is "any help given to learners that assists them in using a specific skill" (Neitzel & Wolery, 2009, p. 1). Prompting is also an essential component of all teaching and something that we do naturally. The challenge is to understand the levels of prompting that we are using, often without thinking about it, and to use them purposefully as part of the teaching and learning process. It is especially important when working to teach social skills to people with ASD to understand how easily they can become dependent on prompts (e.g., being moved to a shared space, told to attend to an object of focus, or handed an item to support self-regulation). Therefore, it is critical that we plan to fade prompts as part of the work that we do each day. Remember too, as you implement an intervention, a verbal prompt is the most difficult prompt to fade!

- **Antecedent-based interventions** describe "a collection of strategies in which environmental modifications are used to change the conditions in the setting that prompt a learner with ASD to engage in an interfering behavior" (Neitzel, 2009, p. 1). These interventions have been used to decrease an identified interfering behavior and increase engagement by modifying the environment (AFIRM Team, 2015). For example, working in a small space while structuring the placement of motivating items can promote successful **ENGAGEMENT**. In addition, identifying and then providing activities that support self-regulation is essential as an individual becomes **READY** to learn.

- **Parent-implemented intervention** describes "parents directly using individualized intervention practices with their child to increase positive learning opportunities and acquisition of important skills. Parents learn to implement practices through a structured parent training program" (Hendricks, 2009, p. 1). The Hanen *More Than Words* program (Sussman, 2012) is an example of a published, evidence-based program designed to teach parents to teach children with ASD communication skills (Reichow, Doehring, Cicchetti, & Volkmar, 2011). Parents are the ultimate skilled partners for facilitating *ENGAGEMENT*. They know their child's joys and challenges and have hearts filled with hope and the desire to engage. Sadly, early attempts to engage their child might have resulted in frustration and deep concern when the child did not have the skills to participate in expected social interaction. It is important to recognize that the problem is not that parents do not know how to be social with their children; rather, children with ASD struggle to know how to be social with their parents. Teaching family members new ways to share space, focus, and pleasure is essential.

- **Visual supports** are "any tool presented visually that supports an individual as he or she moves through the day and can include pictures, written words, objects, arrangement of environment and visual boundaries" (Hume, 2008, p. 1). The use of visual supports is essential for many individuals with ASD, allowing them to understand information using their often more effective visual channel of processing. Visuals also provide information that is concrete and always present, in comparison to the fleeting nature of spoken words. At this stage of learning, visual boundaries can help define the "shared space" and specific objects or pictures can become important items of "shared focus." Later, visual schedules and visual cues will be used to help the learner understand the organization of materials, relevant information, and the instructions for learning.

Case Study: ENGAGEMENT

Meet Jorge

I move in close, uncomfortably close. Jorge glances to the right, while he uses perfect pitch to sing "My Favorite Things." His body is rigid, flexed at the elbows, he holds his shoulders internally rotated, and he wiggles his stiff fingers at mid-line.

He notices the yellow fuzzy pipe cleaner that I hold in his visual field one and one half feet from his eyes. His hands are swift to take it as I hold on and move it toward my face. His eyes do not meet mine but we share a moment. I loosen my grip and he grabs the pipe cleaner and the focus has moved away. Jorge is 15-years-old; he hums and sings but does not speak. He moves in and out of *ENGAGEMENT* throughout his day, depending on the setting, people, and intended focus. Jorge has ASD, he loves to flick objects in his fingers, run quickly forward and backward in an arrhythmical pattern, and eat lemons. His family sees his gifts and gentle spirit.

Jorge slaps his chest a few times, calms, and begins to flick the pipe cleaner. I get in close, choose my moment, and recapture the yellow pipe cleaner. His humming stops, he looks up in my eyes, smiles, and holds the *ENGAGEMENT* for 12 seconds. Someone passes, Jorge loses focus, stoops to get a stick from the ground to flick, and moves away. We spend an hour together entering and exiting and re-entering the world of *ENGAGEMENT*. Self-regulation while sharing the space, focus, and pleasure are skills that will increase the quality of Jorge's life.

In the past three years, I have watched Jorge's moments of *ENGAGEMENT* get longer. These moments happen more frequently and happen with a variety of people. Is it a long process? Yes. Is it meaningful? Yes. *ENGAGEMENT* is the foundation of "being social."

Introducing the Steps to Being Social

We have seen that the foundation of **ENGAGEMENT** is crucial to any consideration of learning to "be social." In fact, when we talk about teaching social skills to individuals with ASD, there is often no shared definition of what is meant to be taught. Consider an Individualized Education Program (IEP) objective that might address a plan to "improve social skills with 80% accuracy." What skills will be addressed and toward what end? Similarly, what does it mean to take turns in conversation in four of five opportunities? When a parent, with good reason, requests a therapy objective for "making friends," what pre-requisite skills are required? The Steps to Being Social are an attempt to answer these questions and provide a road map for moving thoughtfully toward the acquisition of meaningful social skills. At every step, we will see that each sits atop the infrastructure of **ENGAGEMENT**. As individuals advance from one step to the next, you will see that they periodically need to "drop down" and spend some time in the **FOUNDATION** to become self-regulated and re-connected in their ability to share space, focus, and pleasure. Perhaps this can be conceived as an elevator – once organized within the **FOUNDATION**, it is not necessary to climb each step again; rather, individuals can return to the step where they have been working successfully. Consider your own social world and the times that you might need to re-group to return to using your acquired skills in "being social."

The steps are divided into three skill sets: **LOWER 4**, **MIDDLE 4**, and **UPPER 4**. This organization is designed to assist in planning activities for teaching social skills and matching goals to evidence-based practices. These groupings might also be useful in matching individuals when you work on social skills as a part of a group. Let us begin ascending the Steps to Being Social at the **LOWER 4** skill set.

CHAPTER
2

LOWER FOUR

As an individual becomes more frequently engaged for longer periods of time, the **LOWER 4** steps are addressed. Essentially, the **LOWER 4** steps are a time of learning to be together with a social partner and beginning to understand, and indeed be motivated by, reciprocal social interaction. Throughout the model, interaction is defined as a back-and-forth exchange with a social partner. Later, conversation will be defined as a back-and-forth exchange that includes sending and receiving messages with one another. Social partners at all steps of the **LOWER 4** continue to be skilled partners, that is, family members, adult friends, therapists, and teachers who are trained to facilitate social skills. Same-age individuals continue to be motivating role models and trained peers can also begin to teach specific skills near the top of the **LOWER 4**. As you will see, there is a huge development in the **LOWER 4** as a learner progresses from simply noticing that someone is with him in his space to participating in reciprocal exchanges, including a balance of starting the interaction and responding to someone else. As you begin the steps of the **LOWER 4**, remember to assess self-regulation as you approach each moment of "being social"—*Calm + Alert = READY* is the foundation of every social interaction (Kalberg, Laurel, & Taylor, 2013).

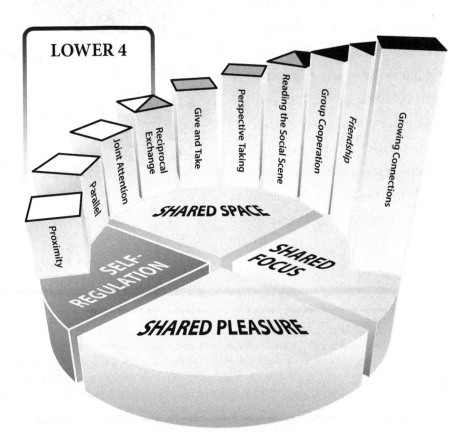

Gabriel will help you get to know the LOWER 4 steps ...

Gabriel is a 26-year-old man with ASD living in a home with three other adult males with developmental disabilities. Gabriel is nonverbal and communicates by using gestures (e.g., nodding or shaking his head), taking a person's hand to something he wants, and occasionally pointing to pictures. Gabriel enjoys hiking, swimming, and shooting basketballs and is most **READY** to socially engage after these activities. He works three mornings per week washing windows at a local gym with the support of a job coach. His interests are colors, specific gas stations, and drinking coffee. Gabriel enjoys his life at home and work and is working hard to share his experiences with others.

LOWER 4: Proximity

Initially, we address proximity as the ability to share the same space as another person, within at least five feet, though perhaps not interacting or engaging in the same activity. This is just one small step above the foundation of **ENGAGEMENT**, as we continue to be concerned with an individual's ability to "be with" another person and begin working to stay in that shared space for longer periods of time. The skilled social partner moves into the social space, calls a small amount of attention to herself, and begins to take actions that are similar to the activities of the individual learner. While it is not important here that the individual is engaging in the same activity or sharing the materials, we look for signs of interest such as reaching, moving near, or vocalizing toward the social partner. When the learner is demonstrating this step, she is able to maintain proximity for at least five minutes.

Gabriel can demonstrate proximity successfully in several environments including: taking the city bus with his caregiver, hanging out at a coffee shop, and working at his window washing job. In all of these environments, he is successful at being within five feet of others and he appears to be aware that others are sharing his space. He shows this by smiling, making specific noises, sitting with people, and moving in and out of proximity with others.

LOWER 4: *Parallel*

As we begin to spend more time in a shared space, we practice being with someone and using the same materials, even if not equally or for the same purpose. Many of you who have experience with young children will recognize this parallel play, where two people engage in the same activity side by side. You will see that as part of this step to "being social," a learner of any age might be developing this skill. We encourage the learner to notice her social partner, perhaps by glancing at what her partner is doing or even smiling as she sees another person doing just what she likes to do. She might also change her expression, indicating awareness that a moment is being shared in a new way. When the learner is demonstrating this step, she will visually attend briefly to what her partner is doing.

Gabriel demonstrates parallel successfully in some environments such as, eating at his home with his roommates; pumping gas; and hiking. In all these environments, he is successful at being within five feet of others and he appears to be aware that others are sharing his space. He glances at others and smiles and looks at the objects others are using. Gabriel's ability to focus on others and realize he is participating in a parallel activity is directly affected by the amount of sensory stimulation in the immediate environment. He is most calm and alert and therefore **READY** after participating in gross motor activities. Gabriel moves on and off this step frequently.

LOWER 4: Joint Attention

Joint attention is a critical skill that describes the ability to coordinate visual attention with a social partner (Mundy & Burnette, 2005). At this step, we begin to see the learner following and/or initiating attention to an item of interest. We teach the learner to follow the social partner's direction, such as a look, point, sound, or word, to attend to something that is known to be of interest to him. We also teach the learner to bring his partner's attention to something of his interest.

To achieve his purpose of sharing attention, he learns to alternate his gaze between an object of interest and his social partner to assure that each is attending and sharing the experience. It is obviously important at this step to have items and actions available that are of great interest to the learner. In addition, the social partner often needs to use big exaggerated actions and expressions and slow down the pace of his sounds, words, and movements to get the attention of the learner. In contrast, we look for and accept any small sign that the learner wants to share his interest with another person.

Gabriel is practicing joint attention successfully for short periods of time at home, work, and in the community. At home, his caregivers set up opportunities to share attention while setting the table for meals. For example, he follows their point to the items needed to set the table. When given time to process, Gabriel will sometimes look at the caregiver, then look at a utensil, and then look back at the caregiver to show proudly that he has done his work correctly. At work, Gabriel will again follow the point of his job coach to wash certain areas of a window. The house and employment staffs are using these opportunities to practice joint attention.

LOWER 4: Reciprocal Exchange

As the learner is able to initiate and respond to an item or activity of joint attention, we begin to focus on back-and-forth interaction, a key component of any meaningful social communication. At this step, the learner begins to orient her body to her social partner. She maintains a shared focus for increasing amounts of time and learns to give and take an object, imitate sounds and actions, wait for her partner to respond, and eventually engage in a reciprocal interaction that lasts for more than one exchange. Interactions can be verbal or nonverbal; the back-and-forth nature of the exchange is key. This crucial step in learning to "be social" is carried into the *MIDDLE 4.*

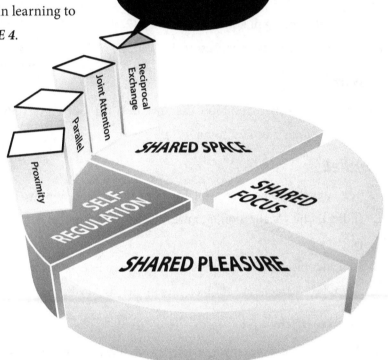

Gabriel is beginning to practice reciprocal exchange for brief periods of time at home and at work. At home, he takes color-matched cards from his caregiver and gives a card when it is the caregiver's turn. At work, he shares a spray bottle with his job coach as each takes a turn spraying the window. He is learning to orient his body to his communication partner in both of these activities and wait with expectation for the activity to continue. He has learned to pass and receive objects during activities that he enjoys, which keeps the interaction going for several exchanges. To make this step successful, the interaction needs to be structured. The space must have visual boundaries, proximity must be close, and the object that is being passed must be interesting to Gabriel. Two partners in the exchange are enough because his ability to wait for a turn is limited. Structure provides Gabriel with an understanding of a clear beginning and end for this challenging work of "being social." It builds trust between Gabriel and his communication partner, helping him understand that he will not be asked to participate in this social activity forever. Setting opportunities for Gabriel to practice these skills with various materials and people, and in a variety of environments, is the key to helping him get to the next step of "being social."

Sub-Skills of LOWER 4

The sub-skills of the **LOWER 4** are the mini-skills needed to be proficient at each **LOWER 4** step. It is important to note that the complexity of social interaction makes it a must to address more than one sub-skill at a time. Measuring the growth of a specific sub-skill, which comes so intuitively to most, is yet again a challenge. In the Steps model, sub-skills of the steps are scored on a 0–3 scale. Remember you are considering these skills in relationship to a Skilled Partner (SP).

The sub-skill is not present.	(0)	
The sub-skill is emerging.	(1)	
The sub-skill is being practiced.	(2)	
The sub-skill is proficient or mastered.	(3)	

0 = Not yet
1 = Beginning
2 = Practicing
3 = Got it

Proximity:

☐ Able to share space (no more than five feet) without aggression or excessive physical contact or vocalizations for at least five minutes

Parallel:

☐ Tolerates skilled partner using the same material within five feet

☐ Indicates by vocalization, gesture, or glance that an SP is using the same material or doing the same activity

☐ Indicates pleasure by smiling or other change in expression

☐ Attends (e.g., looks at action or person) briefly to what the SP is doing

Joint Attention:

☐ Attends to the same object or activity for at least three seconds

☐ Follows SP's direction to attend to an object of the learner's interest

☐ Initiates attention to an object of the learner's interest

☐ Alternates visual attention between object of interest and the SP

Reciprocal Exchange:

☐ Orients body/attends to the SP

☐ Maintains a brief shared focus with the SP

☐ Imitates a sound or action

☐ Takes an offered object

☐ Gives an object and/or directs a sound or action to the SP

☐ Waits with expectation (e.g., maintains body orientation) for a response

☐ Engages in back-and-forth interaction for more than one exchange

Evidence-Based Practices (EBPs) to Support LOWER 4

Several evidence-based strategies have been shown to support the development of social skills and have proven in our own practice to be particularly supportive for teaching the ***LOWER 4***. Keep in mind that evidence-based strategies used for the ***FOUNDATION*** will likely continue to be useful at this stage of teaching.

- **Naturalistic intervention** is "a collection of practices including environmental arrangement, interaction techniques and strategies based on applied behavior analysis; practices use learner interests by building complex skills that are naturally reinforcing and appropriate to a natural interaction" (Franzone, 2009, p. 1). Reinforcement for increasing targeted skills uses items and activities that are intrinsically a part of the interaction. Critically, learning is facilitated in the context of a social relationship and strategies are seen to promote generalization (Schreibman et al., 2015). These interventions are especially effective at the ***LOWER 4*** because they capitalize on a child's motivations and relationships and allow supportive social partners to facilitate skills in the learner's day-to-day life. Strategies are based on following a child's lead in interaction and promoting strong engagement in learning and are often helpful to support "being social" in the context of short, structured back-and-forth interactions.

  - **Joint attention training** is a naturalistic intervention that is often taught to parents. This strategy involves directly teaching the child to coordinate attention between a social partner and an object or event in the environment. Joint attention training has been shown to be very effective in both teaching a learner to respond to a social partner calling attention to something and teaching the learner to initiate coordinated gaze shifting and pointing for a social purpose (Reichow, Doehring, Cicchetti, & Volkmar, 2011). Many families have found that a structured way to share attention with their learner is exciting and highly effective.

- **Discrete trial training** is "a one-to-one instructional approach used to teach skills in a planned, controlled, and systematic manner" (Bogin, 2008, p. 1). This approach is often used when a skill is best taught in small steps with repeated practice. Within the ***LOWER 4***, skills such as following cues to attend to an item, motor and vocal imitation, and giving and taking items are often well taught with planned and repeated practice. Learned skills are then applied to a more naturalistic setting.

Visual supports were defined in the section on ***ENGAGEMENT***. Recognizing that the visual channel of processing is often most efficient for the learner with ASD, at this stage of learning we continue to use visual boundaries (e.g., visually defining the space and materials), as well as visual schedules and visual cues. Visual schedules show the learner where to go and in what order. Schedules can help learners in ***LOWER 4*** go to the place in the room where social interaction is happening. Visual cues are a visual representation of instructions that also help the learner move through the environment successfully. For example, when the learner can see there are three items to pass to a social partner, she knows when the social task is complete (Mesibov, Shea, & Schopler, 2004). Remember that visual supports promote independence in social development as learners climb the steps to "being social."

Sample Activities to Enhance LOWER 4 Skill Sets
Step ... Objective ... Activity

Experience has given us some favorite activities for teaching skills at each step, courtesy of our best teachers, the courageous learners climbing the steps to being social! These are but a few suggested examples of the infinite creative activities that can help support learners as they develop skills. Because learners at each step can be of any age, it is important to consider the age appropriateness of strategies and materials that are created, implemented, and adapted. Furthermore, even as you think deeply about this complex task of learning social skills, remember to be playful and have fun—social skills are all about connecting with other people, and shared pleasure, as we have seen, is the essence of "being social."

The following are examples of activities for an adult (Gabriel) that helped teach the **LOWER 4**. Because many younger learners are working on these **LOWER 4** steps, we have also included sample activities appropriate for a younger learner (Megan, age six).

Step being addressed: Proximity

Sample Objective: At the coffee shop with his caregiver, when presented with a visual timer, Gabriel will stay at the table with his caregiver for at least five minutes in four out of five opportunities.

Sample Activity: Visual Timer

Materials needed: Coffee, timer

Steps for implementation:
1. Sit at table with coffee.
2. Assemble timer in front of Gabriel by placing five poker chips on a vertical board that has a pocket at the bottom (see picture).
3. Remove a poker chip after approximately one minute and put it in pocket at bottom of timer.
4. Continue to remove poker chips at each minute and give verbal praise for staying in the shared space.
5. When all the poker chips are removed and in the pocket at the bottom of the visual timer, Gabriel can walk around the coffee shop.

Step being addressed: Proximity

Sample Objective: During a structured small group activity and when given up to three verbal reminders, Megan will stay in a designated area for seven minutes in four out of five opportunities.

Sample Activity: Space Shapes

Materials needed: Masking or carpet tape

Steps for implementation:

1. Use tape to make shapes on carpet large enough for a child's body to fit.
2. Introduce shapes to all the students with excitement and demonstrate that it is important for their bodies to remain within the space during the activity.
3. Praise children who are keeping their body in the shape.
4. Have students change shapes periodically.

Step being addressed: Parallel

Sample Objective: During structured card game time, after dinner at the group home, with house-mates each playing their own card game, Gabriel will demonstrate that he notices his peers by smiling, looking briefly at a peer, or gesturing toward a peer at least three times during a five-minute activity.

Sample Activity: Game Time

Materials needed: Color card games

Steps for implementation:

1. Gather for game time in one room of the house.
2. Give each participant cards to begin playing.
3. Facilitator uses exaggerated facial expressions, gestures, and sounds to call attention to each person's game.
4. Wait for Gabriel to look up or take notice of the others.
5. After he notices, the facilitator makes a short excited comment and/or facial expression to reinforce Gabriel for looking and gives him an additional color card.

Step being addressed: Parallel

Sample Objective: During a small structured group with no less than three participants engaging in the same activity, Megan will demonstrate that she notices her peers by smiling, looking briefly at a peer, or gesturing toward a peer at least three times during a five-minute activity.

Sample Activity: Bubble Play

Materials needed: Bubbles

Steps for implementation:

1. Get the group in a circle and have learners sit with their bodies facing each other.
2. Begin by blowing bubbles into the group to help the learners focus on the bubbles. Stop blowing the bubbles and move the bubble container and wand near a peer. Wait for Megan to look up or take notice of the peer, then have the peer blow the bubbles.
3. Continue and encourage increased attention to the others who are participating in the activity.

Step being addressed: Joint Attention

Sample Objective: During a structured activity with a skilled partner and given a visual prompt (e.g., looking and pointing), Gabriel will look at an object identified by the skilled partner in four out of five opportunities.

Sample Activity: What's in the grocery bag?

Materials needed: Grocery bag with five food items that Gabriel likes

Steps for implementation:

1. Gabriel and his caregiver stand at the kitchen counter.
2. The caregiver reaches into the grocery bag and shows a highly preferred food item to Gabriel.
3. The caregiver puts the food back into the bag and then looks into the bag and lifts and shakes the bag with a big, excited expression on her face.
4. With large, slow body movements and facial expressions, the caregiver looks at Gabriel and then looks and points into the bag and then looks at Gabriel again.
5. When Gabriel looks at the item with the caregiver, he is given the item to stack on the shelf.

Step being addressed: Joint Attention

Sample Objective: During a structured activity with a skilled partner and given a visual prompt (e.g., looking and pointing), Megan will look at an object identified by the skilled partner in four out of five opportunities.

Sample Activity: What's in the bag?

Materials needed: Bag and a few items of interest

Steps for implementation:

1. Have Megan and the skilled partner (SP) sit close together at the same table.
2. When Megan is settled, the SP reaches into a bag and shows a highly preferred toy to Megan.
3. The SP puts the toy back into the bag and then looks into the bag and lifts and shakes the bag with a big, excited expression on her face.
4. With large, slow body movements and facial expressions, the SP looks at Megan and then looks and points into the bag and then looks at Megan again.
5. When Megan looks at the item with the SP, she is given the item to play with.

Related Reference: Koegel & Koegel (2006)

Step being addressed: Reciprocal Exchange

Sample Objective: During a structured group of no less than three participants and given no more than three physical prompts, Gabriel will participate in three repetitions of taking a handed item, attending to it (by looking) for no less than two seconds, and handing it to another person in four out of five opportunities.

Sample Activity: Gas Station Logos

Materials needed: 10 gas station logo cards, small card box

Steps for implementation:
1. Sit at a table with three peers and job coach.
2. Encourage Gabriel to position his body to face the others in the group.
3. Bring attention to the logo card deck.
4. Give a card to Gabriel and give him 30 seconds to examine the card.
5. Prompt Gabriel to pass the card to the next person and immediately give him another card.
6. When the card gets to the last person, that person puts the card in the box.
7. When all the cards have been passed and placed in the box, the activity is over.
8. Later, change the placement of players so a different person puts the cards in the box.

Step being addressed: Reciprocal Exchange

Sample Objective: During a structured group of no less than three participants and given no more than three physical prompts, Megan will participate in three repetitions of taking a handed item, attending to it (by looking) for no less than two seconds, and handing it to another person in four out of five opportunities.

Sample Activity: Water Bottle Stuff

Materials needed: Any size water bottle filled with at least six small plastic items (e.g., erasers, Legos, animals) placed inside.

Steps for implementation:

1. Have the group sit in a circle with their bodies facing each other.
2. Introduce the bottle and look at the floating items using exaggerated facial expressions. Then pass the bottle to the next person.
3. Support each person in the group to take the bottle, look in the bottle, then orient his/her body to the next person while handing the bottle to the next person. It can help to have an SP in-between the learners. Later, encourage learners to look and point to or label one item in the bottle.
4. Add new objects each time, but leave the favorite items in the bottle.

Case Study: LOWER 4

Meet Chase

Chase enters the room all smiles, following the exact same sequence and pattern he does each week. He passes his visual schedule and glances at the written phrases, no doubt memorizing the entire board faster than I can read it. He goes into the waiting area and notices familiar people in his group but is only drawn to them if they are paired with electronics. At nine-years-old, Chase enjoys pacing while he plays an *Angry Birds* game in his head. If electronics are shared, they hold Chase's attention indefinitely. Without electronics, shared attention to an object, topic, or person is held for only one to two minutes.

Increasing the frequency, duration, and partners for reciprocal exchange is the goal of therapy. We visually show Chase how many pieces are in the activity, which symbolizes how many times he will be going back and forth with his peers, to help him understand how long the activity will continue. The activities Chase loves include tasks with a gross motor component and those that involve humor. We stretch these preferred activities for longer amounts of time, providing additional chances to practice reciprocity. Other activities that are of less interest, such as passing objects while seated or naming and then passing a picture, are completed with fewer repetitions required. In between these exhausting social interactions, therapy includes movement, heavy muscle work activities, and oral motor opportunities such as blowing bubbles into water or using whistles that vibrate. This oral input has consistently helped Chase to stay regulated and **READY** to learn and successfully practice the Steps to Being Social.

Chase notices as the activities are about to end and verbalizes how many repetitions are left. He is beginning to spontaneously engage in back-and-forth activity with his peers and the action itself appears at times motivating. His peers are patient, giving him time to process and not letting Chase charge forward when it is not his turn. He begins to watch and even clap for his peers as he waits for a reciprocal response. As Chase becomes more familiar with the games and social partners, he begins to be motivated by the social experience and not just completing the game. Opportunities to practice this back-and-forth interaction with peers, including important sub-skills such as body orientation, waiting with expectation, and increased attention, are essential to his becoming stronger in these skills and helping him become motivated by the social experience itself.

CHAPTER
3

MIDDLE FOUR

The **MIDDLE 4** also represent a huge leap in the journey toward "being social." The learner who has started to engage in back-and-forth interactions in the **LOWER 4** now grows to use directed communication and understand both that others have different ideas than his own and that there is indeed much social activity happening around him. The learner also begins to understand why he is learning new social behaviors, that is, that his own actions affect his relationships with other people. He learns why specific social skills will help him along his way to "being social." Moving into the **MIDDLE 4,** interactions will continue to be facilitated by a skilled partner; however, trained peers will become an important part of social learning. When thinking about the appropriate social partner, consider back-and-forth social interaction as a game of catch. While the learner is honing his skills to "throw" and "catch" the message, the partner needs to work especially hard to catch the message sent and then carefully throw a message back. Later, the learner can play the game with a variety of partners in a variety of settings. Remember that successful social interaction can only happen in the context of self-regulation. Take time to support the learner to be calm and alert so that he can be **READY** for the "game" of back-and-forth social communication.

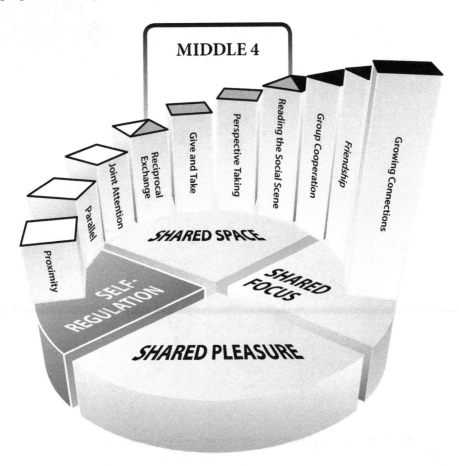

Jessi will help you get to know the MIDDLE 4 steps ...

NASCAR is what Jessi thinks about most of the time. He is a vibrant, energetic, 11-year-old in a general education fourth grade classroom, trying to please his teacher and make one friend. His family notices his "special interest" and certain repeated patterns of behavior, especially when he is stressed. They hope that someday his interests will lead him to employment. For now, they would like for him to feel included with other kids and, yes, to have one friend.

MIDDLE 4: Reciprocal Exchange

While the learner began to engage in reciprocal social interaction during her growth in the **LOWER 4**, she now learns not only to engage in back-and-forth interaction but also to wait for the response of her social partner and to engage in back-and-forth interaction for an increasing number of exchanges. Interactions become more fluid as she begins to anticipate increasing pleasure in being reciprocal with another person. Here the learner finds that many activities can be enjoyed in a back-and-forth exchange.

In a familiar environment, with familiar peers, Jessi, who sometimes struggles with anxiety, is calm and can execute all the sub-skills of reciprocal exchange with any skilled partner. He knows to orient his body and wait for a response. Although Jessi can spontaneously have a back-and-forth interaction with a skilled partner, he is still practicing this with peers. He states that it is "harder to know when to talk with peers - it's hard to figure out when they pause and it's my turn to talk."

MIDDLE 4: *Give and Take of Conversation*

At this step, the learner begins to send and receive messages as part of a social interaction. This can be with or without words. We can think of the message as an intentional direction, request, question, or comment that is clearly directed to another person. Perhaps the learner gives something that he wants to show, points to something that he wants to have, or names something that catches his interest. In turn, he begins to respond when his social partner sends a message to him. In addition, he learns strategies to limit the number of turns he takes based on the social situation and his communication partner and can maintain attention within the conversation for longer periods of time. When the learner is demonstrating this step, he can engage in a spontaneous back-and-forth conversation (i.e., messages sent back and forth with or without words) on a shared topic for at least three exchanges.

During the give and take of conversation, Jessi will respond to a peer or skilled partner but he needs time to process the language and formulate a response. He has learned through practice to direct the message to a person, though this does not always look fluid or comfortable. Jessi is practicing the spontaneous back and forth of a shared topic, but sometimes he likes to pull it back to his own interest, such as specific video games or NASCAR.

MIDDLE 4: Perspective Taking

This step of Perspective Taking is an often-discussed aspect of social communication related to ASD (Winner, 2009). Perspective taking requires abilities related to the theory of mind (ToM) and executive functioning (EF). Baron-Cohen, Leslie, and Frith described ToM as a person's ability to consider another person's point of view. The lack of this skill is sometimes referred to as "mindblindness" (Baron-Cohen, Leslie, & Frith, 1985; Baron-Cohen, 1997). Winner (2009) stated, "Without ToM, social development falters or is halted altogether" (p. 3). Executive functioning includes skills such as, organizing, planning, sequencing, sustaining attention, and inhibiting responses (Myles & Southwick, 2005). Self-monitoring is also an important aspect of executive functioning. These skills are essential for learning to understand the perspective of others.

At this step, the learner begins to be aware that others have different thoughts than she does and is able to comment about what other people might be thinking. As she demonstrates an understanding of this very important concept, she begins to identify ways to figure out what other people are thinking by reading cues that can be both verbal

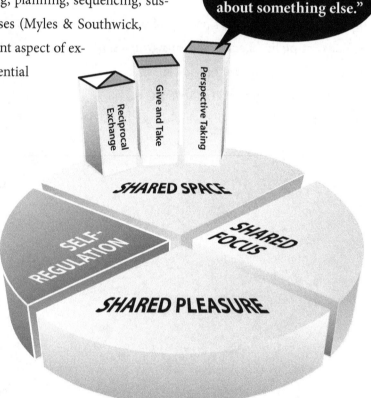

Through line-drawn pictures on a white board, Jessi began to verbalize what he was having thoughts about and to understand that other people's thoughts were different than his. He now practices this skill across settings, both with a skilled partner and with trained peers. Jessi has learned what parts of the face are important to read and watch to make a guess at what someone is thinking such as, the eyes, eye brows and mouth (Winner, 2007). He has been told that his facial expression is often the same, not reflecting his thoughts and feelings. He works to consciously make his face have certain expressions that he practices when he brushes his teeth at night. Using appropriate facial expressions is labored and awkward. He is also learning to read the facial expressions of others and states, "I am not caught by surprise so much now!" Jessi is just beginning to understand that he can put thoughts about NASCAR on "pause" and therefore not make car sounds with his throat, so that other kids at recess will not respond negatively to him. Perspective taking has been a big leap of learning for Jessi and he is beginning to show a greater interest in others and how they see the world.

and nonverbal. In addition, she starts to realize that what other people think has an impact on her own feelings. Later in the *UPPER 4*, on the step of Group Cooperation, she will work to change her own behavior based on what another person is thinking and how she feels about it.

MIDDLE 4: Reading the Social Scene

This crucial aspect of "being social" involves noticing what is happening in a social environment, attending to what is relevant, and finding a way to be a part of a social situation. Initially, the learner begins to label the actions that he sees going on around him. He works to attend for a long enough time to choose an aspect of the "social scene" that he wants to be a part of. As he is able to label and attend, he learns to discriminate relevant social information (e.g., who is in the environment and what exactly people are doing together) and eventually to successfully join a social interaction. A very important component of this step is that as the learner is able to attend to important social cues, he begins to feel less overwhelmed about the social environment— he has a chance to notice and make sense of the social world and therefore "step in" with more confidence (Rydell & Treharne, 2015). As he participates, he learns to adjust his social communication based on the social situation and social partners. This last step of the *MIDDLE 4* is quite complex and carries into the *UPPER 4*.

When Jessi is interacting with a skilled partner and is asked about the social scene and given time to respond, he can practice all the sub-skills for this step, including noticing what is happening around him, picking out the interesting people and activities, and adjusting his social behavior in the group. With a peer in a new environment, his anxiety goes up, his repetitive routines get lengthier and more intense, and he has difficulty reading the social scene around him. He has difficulty making a choice, finding the relevant information, and feeling like he belongs.

Sub-Skills of MIDDLE 4

The sub-skills of the ***MIDDLE 4*** are the mini-skills needed to be proficient at the ***MIDDLE 4*** steps. As in the ***LOWER 4***, we usually target several sub-skills as part of one intervention. The skills are again rated on the 0-3 scale described in the ***LOWER 4*** and are now coded in relationship to both a Skilled Partner (SP) and/or a Trained Peer (TP).

The sub-skill is not present. (0)

The sub-skill is emerging. (1)

The sub-skill is being practiced. (2)

The sub-skill is proficient or mastered. (3)

0 = Not yet
1 = Beginning
2 = Practicing
3 = Got it

Reciprocal Exchange:

☐ Orients body/attends to the SP/TP

☐ Maintains a brief shared focus with the SP/TP

☐ Imitates a sound or action

☐ Takes an offered object

☐ Gives an object and/or directs a sound or action to the SP/TP

☐ Waits with expectation (maintains body orientation) for a response

☐ Engages in back-and-forth interaction for more than one exchange

Give and Take of Conversation:

☐ Verbally or nonverbally responds to a message

☐ Intentionally directs a message (nonverbal or verbal)

☐ Matches facial expression to verbal communication or intended meaning

☐ Engages in back-and-forth conversation on a topic (at least three full exchanges)

Perspective Taking:

☐ Indicates by a word or action an understanding that others can have different thoughts (e.g., questions, comments, or facial expressions related to someone else's feelings)

☐ Response or lack of response that indicates an acceptance that others can have different thoughts

☐ Identifies ways to figure out what others are thinking by reading nonverbal cues (e.g., tone, facial expressions, body language)

☐ Communicates that what others think has an impact on personal feelings

Reading the Social Scene

- ☐ Labels the social interactions within a given environment
- ☐ Attends to social situations for enough time to choose whether to join
- ☐ Joins a social interaction
- ☐ Demonstrates methods to cope with nervousness and/or distress related to social performance (e.g., takes deep breaths, walks away, asks for help)
- ☐ Adjusts social communication based on social situation and partners

Evidence-Based Practices (EBPs) to Support MIDDLE 4

The following EBPs can support the development of social skills related to the *MIDDLE 4*. Again, all of the strategies already addressed can still be used on the journey of "being social."

- **Social Skills Training** is "used to teach individuals with ASD ways to appropriately interact with typically developing peers" (Collet-Klingenberg, 2009, p. 1). Groups are small, consisting of two to eight learners with a facilitator. Typically, social groups consist of instruction, role-playing, or practice and feedback to promote positive social interactions with peers. This strategy is especially helpful as learners in the *MIDDLE 4* begin to practice conversation and learn perspective taking skills.

- **Social Narratives** are "interventions that describe social situations in some detail by highlighting relevant cues and offering examples of appropriate responding" (Collet-Klingenberg & Franzone, 2008, p. 1). This intervention is often useful to help learners adjust to changes in routine and change behavior based on cues in a specific situation. Social narratives are individualized and short, often use pictures, and can include social scripts, power cards, and cartoons. This has been a key teaching strategy for us in supporting learners to walk up the steps of the *MIDDLE 4*. Carol Gray developed the "social story" and a wealth of information related to use of this important tool (www. carolgraysocialstories.com).

- **Video Modeling** "uses video recording to provide a visual model of the targeted behavior or skill" (Franzone & Collet-Klingenberg, 2008, p. 1). Videos can be created showing a third person engaging in a target behavior or highlight the learner demonstrating a target skill. Social skills in the *MIDDLE 4* can be broken into smaller steps, such as participation in structured conversation or noticing one part of the social scene, and then viewed one skill at a time. The video model is often viewed prior to practicing a target social skill.

- **Peer Mediated Instruction and Intervention** is "used to typically teach developing peers ways to interact with and help learners with ASD acquire new social skills" (Neitzel, 2008, p. 1). Trained peers, who have been taught specific strategies for supporting the learner, can be highly effective teachers at this stage of social learning. In the *MIDDLE 4*, trained peers can represent a remarkable bridge for learners with ASD to increasing social opportunities with peers in the natural social environment.

Sample Activities to Enhance MIDDLE 4 Skill Sets

Step ... Objective ... Activity

Climbing the steps of the *MIDDLE 4*, we have another list of favorite sample activities that have been developed and adapted with extraordinary learners over the years. As ever, age-appropriate strategies that are delivered with respect, care, and excitement are a key piece of teaching the "steps to being social."

Step being addressed: Reciprocal Exchange

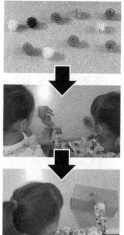

Sample Objective: In a group of no more than five learners, Jessi will follow group instructions to face a peer, take an item from a peer, and pass it to another peer as part of a social game no less than five times in four out of five opportunities.

Sample Activity: Group Put-In

Materials needed: 10 objects that will all fit in one container with a lid and a hole in the lid

Steps for implementation:

1. Get the group members in a line, sitting or standing with their bodies close enough to pass an object to each other. It is best to place skilled partners or trained peers in-between participants to begin this task and teach the routine.
2. Place all the objects at one end of the line and the container at the other end.
3. Model passing an object, one at a time, to the next person down the line and having the last person put the object in the container through the hole in the lid.
4. As the group gets the idea of the routine, fade the skilled partners out of the line and have the participants pass objects to each other.
5. Slow down the pass and increase the distance between group members so that they need to pay more attention and orient their bodies to the peer next to them for a longer period of time.
6. To make this more difficult, try it in a circle or across an even longer distance with an increased number of objects.

Step being addressed: *Give and Take of Conversation*

Sample Objective: During a paired activity and given visual prompts, Jessi will respond to and direct three statements about the identified topic with a trained peer in four out of five opportunities.

Sample Activity: Structured Conversation

Materials needed: Two people, visual conversation sheet, six "talk tokens," 10 pictured scenes (topics)

conversation sheet

topic photos

Steps for implementation:

1. Pair one learner with one trained peer.
2. Set the visual conversation sheet between the learner and peer and place the topic picture on the conversation sheet in the thought bubble—this will be the topic of this short, structured conversation.
3. Give the learner and peer three "talk tokens" each (different color tokens assigned to each person).
4. Instruct the learner and peer to begin a conversation about the identified topic; with each statement, they stack one "talk token" on the talk bubble of the conversation sheet, resulting in a pile of alternating colors.
5. The conversation partners send messages back and forth related to the topic picture until they are out of "talk tokens."
6. Increase the number of "talk tokens" and change the topic photos as skills improve.

thought bubble

talk bubble
talk token

conversation sheet

Step being addressed: Perspective Taking

Sample Objective: In a small group and when presented with images of people in social scenes (e.g., picture, video, or role play), Jessi will verbally identify five ideas that others may be thinking, based on the scene in four out of five opportunities.

Sample Activity: Thought Bubbles

Materials needed: Pictured scenes with characters using various facial expressions while engaging in various social activities. Small white index cards with thought bubbles on them.

Steps for implementation:

1. Sit in a group around a table facing each other.
2. The facilitator picks up a picture and describes the social scene.
3. Every participant is given a small card with an empty thought bubble.
4. The facilitator places the social scene picture in the middle of the table.

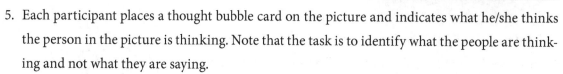

5. Each participant places a thought bubble card on the picture and indicates what he/she thinks the person in the picture is thinking. Note that the task is to identify what the people are thinking and not what they are saying.
6. The facilitator remains in the group to give feedback.
7. After each participant has had a turn, the facilitator can highlight that there are many correct responses. Acknowledge that all participants may be thinking something different and this is okay—the idea is to begin to understand that everyone has different thoughts!

Related Reference: https://www.socialthinking.com/Articles?name=Teaching%20through%20 Thought%20Bubbles%20and%20Talking%20Bubbles

Step being addressed: Reading the Social Scene

Sample Objective: On the playground and when given the verbal prompt "look around," Jessi will verbally identify at least two social activities going on around him in four out of five opportunities.

Sample Activity: What's happening here?

Materials needed: Playground, paper, pencil

Steps for implementation:

1. Take the group out to the playground during recess.
2. Instruct participants to "look around" and write or draw three social activities that they see going on around them for five minutes.
3. Bring the group together to share observations.
4. Later, participants can circle the activity they wish to join.

Case Study: MIDDLE 4

Meet Mason

Mason and I are at the baseball field for the third week in a row. I seek Mason out in the stands wondering what he thinks about spending his spring evenings watching his brother play baseball with my son. "Hey, there's a lot going on here," I comment with the hope of getting a response. After an awkward amount of time, I hear, "Not so much. There's us and them." We begin the give and take of conversation, and while it is slightly labored and requires intermittent wait periods, we discuss the variety of social scenes that are happening around us. Mason looks awestruck, as if he had never taken notice of the scene: all of the people not playing ball, the conversations happening in the stands, the activities of the children on the grass in front of us, and all the events that surround the baseball game he had come to watch. At 17 years old with an IQ and ACT score higher than most, and, oh yes, a diagnosis of ASD, Mason does not need another adult telling him what to "take part" in. What Mason needs is help in noticing social options. He needs time to process and support to problem solve what options might be the most fun for him. Mason needs to recognize his social choices and then have the confidence and skills to join in the social scene that most motivates him.

As the innings go on and the baseball continues, I comment in a compassionate but clear and concrete manner to Mason on the social scene happening around us: "Wow, those kids are kicking that soccer ball," "I see those guys doing their homework at the picnic table," "Those four adults are talking about hunting," "I see those kids playing a pretend game with the Legos they brought from home."

With time, Mason responds thoughtfully, expressing his interest in Legos. We talk about the Lego group, then the conversation moves to the Lego movie and what Lego structure he is building at home. I state that I bet these kids would be impressed with his structure at home and he agrees and smiles.

The next time I see Mason at a game he is sitting in a new place, actually closer to where the Lego kids were the week before. Were they there now? No. Was he ready and waiting for them with a photo on his phone of his Lego structure? Yes. Would it go smoothly when he saw them next? I dearly hoped so. However, the point is that he was given the social information in a way that made sense, and then he made a choice to join a social scene. The following week I arrive to find Mason standing with four kids around him peering at his phone. He saw the choices.

CHAPTER

4

UPPER FOUR

The **UPPER 4**, when arrived at in small steps of structured learning, are the logical final steps to long-lasting, meaningful relationships that are the work of every person's lifetime. The learner, who began to notice the social environment during the **MIDDLE 4**, now sees the social possibilities around him and is able to choose and join an ongoing social interaction. Here he begins to develop skills for being part of a group, including learning to adjust his own behavior in relation to the way others think about him, to help him be successful in group interaction (Winner, 2007). Social partners are now primarily trained peers and, over time, a variety of people in his day-to-day environment. He continues to benefit from coaching and corrective feedback, especially in new social situations, and from opportunities to practice and refine learned skills. Although this is an exciting time to see the possibilities of being "part of a group," in our experience parents have reported that this level of learning can also bring about nervousness. This distress is related to social situations and can inhibit the learner's ability to perform the **UPPER 4** skills. Developing strategies for coping with greater social demands is therefore especially important at this level. As the learner emerges with the skills to develop and sustain relationships, he might reflect on the many steps and the incredibly hard work of his courageous journey.

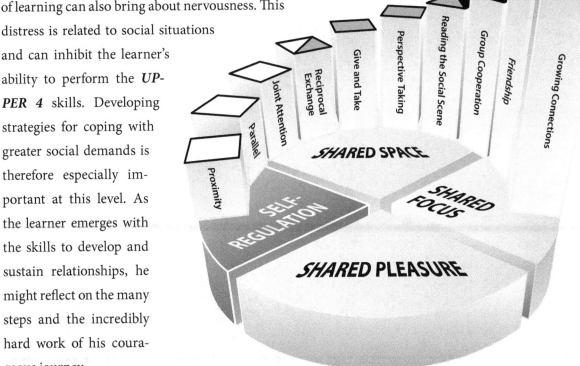

"Team Talk" will help you get to know the UPPER 4 steps ...

This group of five teens is having a variety of middle school experiences. With a range of diagnoses, including ASD, these teens have worked together in a structured sensory/social group for two years. They are now participating in a community-based group to help them practice the **UPPER 4** skill set in the real world with a bit of support. These five are incredible teachers, each with a tremendous drive to belong and be included in this, sometimes, not so friendly social world. These are the kids who are paving the way for so many more—those who can and cannot speak for themselves—to help the world become a bit more open to a variety of social learners.

UPPER 4: *Reading the Social Scene*

The learner began to notice the social environment and find ways to engage in social interactions within that environment while stepping up in the *MIDDLE 4*. Now he is becoming more confident and independent in his ability to scan and notice the social opportunities and find his own place in the social scene.

As described in the *MIDDLE 4*, emerging confidence in understanding the social scene can help decrease anxiety about "being social." Now, in the *UPPER 4*, the learner can begin to develop independent coping strategies to use when social stress makes it difficult to continue to practice and participate. He is able to change his own social behavior based on where he is and who he is engaging with. Critically, he begins to use this skill on his own and with similar-age peers in his natural environment.

"Hey, there's a lot going on here!"

Reading the Social Scene

SHARED SPACE

SELF-REGULATION

SHARED FOCUS

SHARED PLEASURE

In their structured therapy group, these teens had mastered reading the social scene. They knew what was happening around them and who was doing what. They made choices and joined in the activities that were motivating. Each one took great pride, or pain, in telling the facilitator what was not motivating. However, out in the world, in the community pool, the park, one another's homes, or the movie theater, use of learned skills became more difficult. It was as if they needed to go back to **ENGAGEMENT**, specifically self-regulation (Calm + Alert = **READY**) to help them have successful social interactions. Then and only then could they access the skills they had previously learned.

UPPER 4: *Group Cooperation*

At this step, the learner is able to orient her body and focus within a small group of people and is working to be able to express her desire to be a part of that group. She learns to stay on a structured topic, especially when that topic is made clear to her, and adjust her own ideas to be a group participant. As her enjoyment of the social interaction grows, she is flexible enough to participate in a topic or activity that was chosen by somebody else. In addition, she learns to comfortably end a social interaction. All of this requires a growing ability in the area of executive functioning, previously discussed in the **MIDDLE 4**. The learner needs to have an idea of joining a group, make a plan to join and follow through with those plans. This is an extraordinarily complex time of growth, when the learner understands more clearly that she is not just with the group but indeed is a part of the group. Along with this evolving perception, the learner begins to understand not only that other people have different thoughts than her own, but also that her own behavior can affect the thoughts and feelings of other people. Critically, she starts to sort out why she might want to be perceived in a different way and how to adjust her own behavior to maintain membership in a group. As these important skills develop, the learner is guided to reflect on her own behavior and to identify and then repair social "mistakes" by adjusting her own behavior. She is able to use supports developed in earlier steps to practice these skills with a variety of peers in her environment.

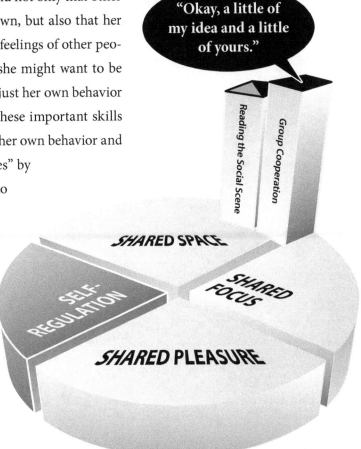

Each one of these participants wants to be in the group, yet how they show that looks different. The courage it takes for each of them to move through their distress about belonging and "not messing up" is a lesson we all could learn. A few have "got it" in the area of physically staying in their own space and with the group. A few others are "practicing" this skill, still sometimes invading others' space and /or orbiting around the action when the sensory stimulation becomes too much. One participant is so challenged by his distractibility that he is at the "beginning" stage of this skill, requiring many prompts to be physically with the group. When each teen picks his/her own topic, they are well able to stay on that topic. When the facilitator or another group member picks the topic, it's a challenge to stay engaged. The facilitator needs to identify the topic. She also provides visual cues to help the teens understand how long they can talk and to decrease interruptions. As Ian and Elsa so brilliantly put it: "We know how to do the back-and-forth thing when it's just us two, but with more, it's way harder." This entire group is at the "beginning" and "practicing" stage of changing their own behaviors in order to be part of a group. They complement each other in this way: Elsa needs to stop talking while Katy needs to talk more. Ian needs to not give in so much while Logan needs to give in a bit more. Missy needs to be okay with a bit of touch while Katy needs to stop touching everyone. They are a group, on a path to becoming more flexible. Sometimes the activity and topic lead the members to "being social," sometimes they dig in their heels with frustration and sometimes nervousness prevents them from even coming to try out these skills.

UPPER 4: *Friendship*

At last, we arrive at the place where so many individuals with ASD and their family members longed to be from the start. Friendships are a key component in the life of many individuals and help us to develop our social and emotional skills (Benton, Hollis, Mahler, & Womer, 2011). The learner who needs support to de-

velop skills for making friends starts by noticing that another person has similarities to him (e.g., specific interests or experiences). He then must understand that even while friends might have much in common, they will also have differences that must be accepted if not understood. He must accept that people can have more than one friend. In today's world, learners must also develop skills to use social media appropriately, based on age, setting, and social context. When the learner is demonstrating this step, he is able to make plans to spend time with a friend in more than one setting.

"I can't wait to get home and see my friends, you know the ones on my 'play station,' I don't have any real live friends." This makes these kids sad, and their parents devastated! Yet this group is learning the skills of friendship. They know what they have in common. They work, rework, and battle over having more than one friend in their group at a time and are beginning to understand the difference between friends and acquaintances. They sometimes still rely on their families to set friendship opportunities for them. They need facilitators to help them figure out how to problem solve when people don't follow the social rules they have worked so hard to learn. They need to overcome and work through the fear that sometimes holds them captive to their rooms and electronics, which are so predictable, reliable, and forgiving.

UPPER 4: *Growing Connections*

This last step represents the life-long work of maintaining a relationship over time, distance, and changing circumstances. For learners with ASD, it is important to keep in mind that just as in the earlier steps of learning, we need to teach explicitly the "rules" that govern adult relationships, including understanding the importance of hygiene routines, behaviors that are appropriate or not appropriate in various contexts, and consent between social partners (Beytien, 2011, 2016). In addition, adults continue to need strategies for self-regulation to be ***READY*** to sustain these growing connections. As the learner develops her skills, she understands various types of friendships and personal boundaries and safety. She is able to state differences in various levels of intimacy and make safe choices based on that understanding. She can state her own role in personal relationships and conflicts that arise. Being proficient at this step is where most adults aim to be socially, but we honor each learner's individual path and abilities on the unique journey to "being social."

"We are in it for the long haul."

Reading the Social Scene

Group Cooperation

Friendship

Growing Connections

SHARED SPACE

SHARED FOCUS

SELF-REGULATION

SHARED PLEASURE

The "Team Talk" group members are not here yet, but they will be some day. For now, they are able to express their hopes for future relationships. Adults tell us there are many challenges to this step, with or without a diagnosis of ASD. This helps us understand the importance of learning the critical skills at each step along the way.

Sub-Skills of UPPER 4

The **UPPER 4** encompass sub-skills that are also targeted in groups. The scoring of 0–3 is used only with trained peers as the learner moves toward the generalization of these skills.

The sub-skill is not present.	(0)	0 = Not yet
The sub-skill is emerging.	(1)	1 = Beginning
The sub-skill is being practiced.	(2)	2 = Practicing
The sub-skill is proficient or mastered.	(3)	3 = Got it

Reading the Social Scene:

☐ Labels the social interactions within a given environment

☐ Attends to social situations for enough time to choose whether to join

☐ Joins the social interaction

☐ Demonstrates methods to cope with nervousness and/or distress related to social performance (e.g., deep breaths, walks away, asks for help)

☐ Adjusts social communication based on social situation and partners

Group Cooperation:

☐ Expresses desire to be part of a group

☐ Physically stays with the group and in own personal space

☐ Agrees on a topic or activity (e.g., suggests, negotiates)

☐ Participates when a topic/activity is chosen by someone else

☐ Appropriately breaks from or ends the interaction

☐ Recognizes that personal behavior affects the thoughts and feelings of others

☐ Identifies and repairs a social mistake

☐ Adjusts behavior based on the thoughts and feelings of others to be a part of the group

Friendship:

☐ Finds out what he/she has in common with another person

☐ Accepts things that are not in common

☐ Accepts that people can have more than one friend

☐ Appropriately uses social media

☐ Makes a plan to be with a friend (e.g., time, place, activity)

☐ Spends time together in more than one setting

Growing Connections:

- ☐ States differences in the types of friendship (e.g., best friend, girlfriend)
- ☐ States what information is typically shared in different types of relationships
- ☐ Maintains relationships over time
- ☐ Sustains relationships across distance
- ☐ States differences in various levels of intimacy
- ☐ States his/her own role in social relationships and conflicts
- ☐ Makes safe choices based on level of intimacy

Evidence-Based Practices (EBPs) to Support UPPER 4

At the *UPPER 4*, the learner will continue to benefit from many of the evidence-based strategies previously described. In particular, practices that were discussed in earlier sections that might be helpful to re-visit include:

- **FOUNDATION:** Task Analysis, Reinforcement, Antecedent-based Intervention, and Visual Supports (pp. 12–14)

- **LOWER and MIDDLE 4:** Visual Supports, Social Skill Training, Social Narratives, Video Modeling, and Peer-mediated Instruction and Intervention (pp. 25–26 and 45)

In addition, we have found *Self-Management* to be an excellent strategy to promote skill development and independence. Self-management interventions "help learners with ASD learn to independently regulate their own behaviors and act appropriately in a variety of home, school and community-based situations" (Busick, 2009, p. 1). Teaching often focuses on discriminating between "appropriate" and "inappropriate" behaviors for a given social situation with the learner monitoring and recording targeted social behaviors and rewarding him or herself for meeting social goals.

Sample Activities to Enhance UPPER 4 Skill Sets

Step ... Objective ... Activity

Finally, we come to sample activities to support the **UPPER 4**. While skills at this level are more complex, you might be teaching them to individuals of various ages, pre-school through adulthood. Creating age-appropriate and fun strategies that promote strong learning opportunities will assist in the journey of "being social." Look to the learners to let you know if the activity is meaningful.

Step being addressed: Reading the Social Scene

Sample Objective: In a small group of at least three participants and given a visual prompt (e.g., individualized calming card), Katy will choose from a list of three calming activities and demonstrate use of that strategy in four out of five opportunities.

Sample Activity: Calming Card

Materials needed: Index card with a written list of individually identified calming strategy choices

Steps for implementation:

1. Facilitate a familiar structured social activity.
2. If Katy appears distressed (e.g., twirls hair, stops talking, and/or looks away from the group and action), facilitator prompts her to look at her "calming card."
3. Katy chooses one of the identified calming strategies (e.g., drawing for three minutes, five deep breaths, or getting a drink of water).
4. Katy uses the strategy and returns to the group activity.

Step being addressed: Group Cooperation

Sample Objective: During a structured group of no less than three participants, Elsa will demonstrate at least three group cooperation sub-skills (e.g., negotiate, participate in another participant's topic, break or end an interaction, recognize that her own behavior affects the thoughts and feelings of others, adjusts behaviors based on thoughts and feelings) in four out of five opportunities.

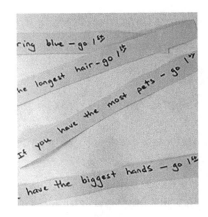

Sample Activity: Who goes first?

Materials needed: Cards with statements describing who would go first in a given activity and any game that requires an order of participation

Steps for implementation:

1. Get the group in a circle, sitting or standing with their bodies facing each other.
2. Ask one participant to pick a statement card (describing who will go first in that activity) from a deck in the middle.
3. Have that participant read the card out loud and instruct the group to follow the directions.
4. Facilitator uses body language to help the participants work together (e.g., looking at her own hand for size and comparing with one other person's hand).
5. Praise students for using the specific sub-skills of Group Cooperation.
6. If participants are having trouble listening and are interrupting each other, call a "freeze" (this is a common word used by teachers and recreational staff that means everyone should stop their body, hold their position, and look at the speaker for further information) and state what you want to happen (e.g., "Look at your hand, put your hand up to somebody else's, compare").

Step being addressed: Friendship

Sample Objective: During a structured group of at least three participants and given a chart for organizing a plan, the group will complete a plan that each member agrees to in four out of five opportunities.

Sample Activity: Plan to Get Together

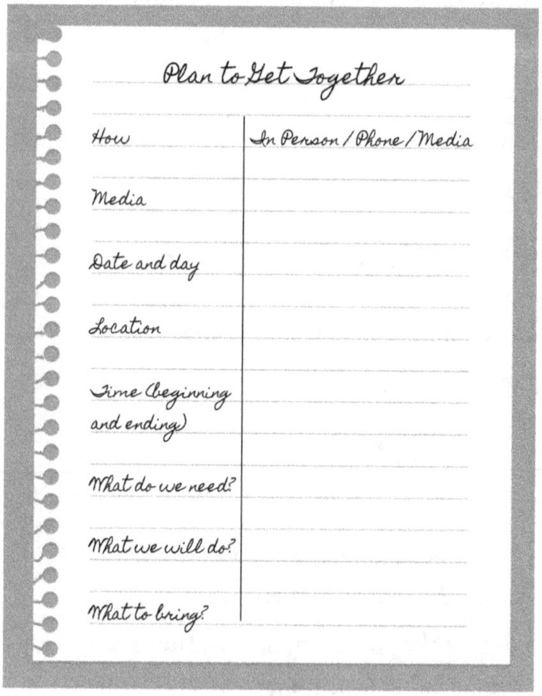

Materials needed: Paper and pen, "Plan to get together" chart

Steps for implementation:

1. Get together in a group with participants standing or sitting and show the group the "Plan the get together" chart.

2. Review the sub-skills of friendship and ask participants to use these skills as they fill out the plan together. Facilitate the group to start at the top and move down the chart.

3. If they are having trouble listening and are interrupting, call a "freeze" and re-state the instructions with prompts to support the use of learned skills.

4. Facilitate the group to move through this process fairly quickly so group members learn the steps, and then fade your assistance.

5. Option: Facilitator videos the process and the group reviews, noting positive sub-skills used.

Chart (handwritten):

Plan to Get Together

How	In Person / Phone / Media
Media	
Date and day	
Location	
Time (beginning and ending)	
What do we need?	
What we will do?	
What to bring?	

Step being addressed: Growing Connections

Sample Objective: During an individual session, Sammy will identify verbally and in writing at least four concrete ways to "stay safe" on a college campus.

Sample Activity: Visual Organizer

Materials needed: Paper and pen/white board and marker

Steps for implementation:

1. Briefly explain to Sammy the need to know what to look for to stay safe on campus.
2. Brainstorm ideas that could help a person stay safe and record on "visual organizer."
3. Ask Sammy to put a star by the ideas she will use.
4. Direct Sammy to take a picture of the "visual organizer" with her phone and save the photo.

Visual Organizer

Case Study: UPPER 4

Meet Andy

Andy marches into his Montessori classroom ready for the morning routine. He scans the room to see what his classmates have selected and decides on the dinosaur book, again. Andy is six-years-old and has recently received a diagnosis of ASD. He appears to want to join the group activity of creating a structure with K'NEX, but there is no teacher helping out. Andy notices that when there is no teacher, kids do not follow the rules and this makes him mad. Andy appears to feel the need to teach the rules and "police" his peers. His teacher has told him that other kids do not appreciate this. Learning and practicing the sub-skills of group cooperation is the focus of Andy's school day and his in-class occupational therapy (OT) session. Andy has practiced four ideas to help him stay calm and ready to play with his friends. He presses his hands together, asks for a three-minute break, chews a large piece of gum, or rolls his pencil in his palms to the count of 20—these ideas help support him to be calm and alert and therefore **READY** to participate.

When I come in for his in-class OT session, the students are directed to switch activities and one group begins to talk about dinosaurs. Now Andy is very motivated to join the group discussion and play. Two of the participants start to walk like a T-rex, which makes Andy extremely frustrated because they have their facts incorrect. The frustration builds quickly and Andy is unable to stop himself from blurting out, "That is not how T-rex dinosaurs walk!" The others stop and stare. I redirect Andy to an area of the room designated to take a break and get regulated. After he is calm and quiet for a countdown of 20 fingers, I hand Andy the social story titled, "When things don't go MY way" (www.carolgraysocialstories.com). We read the words together and look at the pictures. Andy becomes calm, the story is read one more time, and he takes a breath and returns to the class on the carpet. The teacher brings out a can of Popsicle sticks labeled with each student's name. The teacher picks four sticks and reads the names off slowly. These will be the students chosen to act out the dinosaur story. Yes, another opportunity for practicing learned skills! I quickly get the social story and turn it to the page of ideas to use when "you don't get your way." Andy is not picked. He squeezes the book, clenches his teeth, and closes his eyes, but he remains sitting in the group and does not yell out a negative comment to those who were picked. I get a small dinosaur sticker from my pocket and give it to Andy and he puts it on the back of the story. This is a motivator for the effort he used to adjust his behavior to be part of the group.

CHAPTER

5

ASSESSMENT

The STEPS Assessment

The Steps to Being Social help us identify the social skills needed to "get along." The STEPS Assessment helps us know where an individual is on the steps and how to support his or her progress.

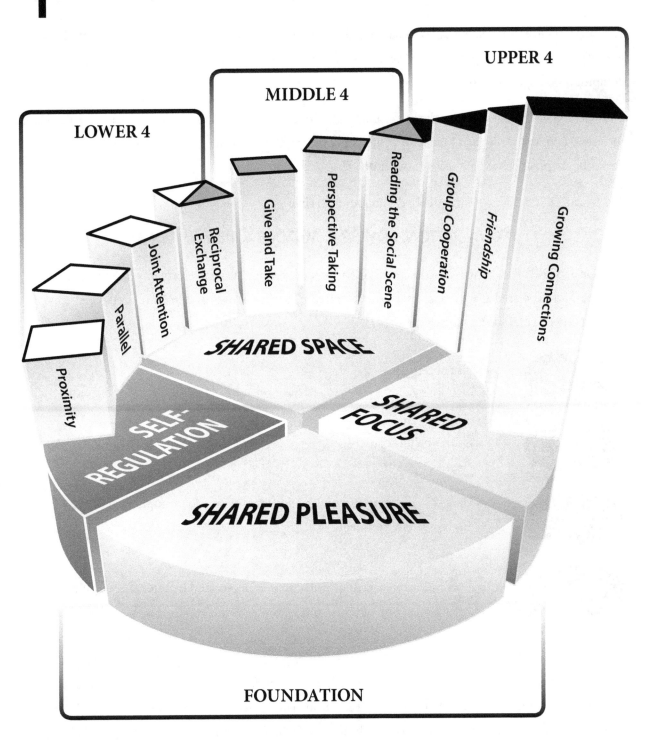

UPPER 4

MIDDLE 4

LOWER 4

Growing Connections

Friendship

Group Cooperation

Reading the Social Scene

Perspective Taking

Give and Take

Reciprocal Exchange

Joint Attention

Parallel

Proximity

SHARED SPACE

SHARED FOCUS

SELF-REGULATION

SHARED PLEASURE

FOUNDATION

Name: _____ DOE: _____ DOB: _____

Evaluator: _____ Setting: _____ Time period: _____

Introduction

The Social STEPS Assessment is not separate from intervention but instead it is a fully integrated part of identifying social challenges, developing solutions, and understanding where to begin as we tackle the complex task of teaching social skills.

The Social STEPS Assessment helps us visualize the progression of social skills from basic Engagement to Friendship and Growing Connections. It points out gaps in critical skills and identifies links to evidence-based practices to help teach those skills.

The Social STEPS Assessment is divided into four skill sets:

FOUNDATION, LOWER 4, MIDDLE 4, and UPPER 4

The Social STEPS Assessment is scored YES or NO when working in the components of ENGAGEMENT (self-regulation, shared space, shared focus, and shared pleasure). Scores of 0 to 3 are used when working on the *LOWER*, *MIDDLE* and *UPPER 4*.

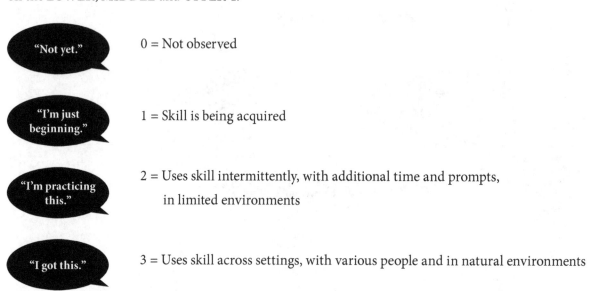

"Not yet."   0 = Not observed

"I'm just beginning."   1 = Skill is being acquired

"I'm practicing this."   2 = Uses skill intermittently, with additional time and prompts, in limited environments

"I got this."   3 = Uses skill across settings, with various people and in natural environments

The skills in the *FOUNDATION* and *LOWER 4* level are designed to be taught by a Skilled Partner (SP), often a family member or a professional. An SP has high motivation for interaction and proficiency for the targeted skills. Moving into the *MIDDLE 4*, the STEPS are also facilitated with Trained Peers (TP); a Trained Peer is any other similar-age person who is taught skills to facilitate specific aspects of "being social."

ENGAGEMENT

ENGAGEMENT is the Foundation to All Social Skills.

Score: | Yes | *or* | No |

Being with a Skilled Partner (SP)

Self-Regulation: Calm + Alert = READY to Learn

☐ Appears to be in control of body and emotions: Stays in designated space without aggression, yelling, or overt signs of distress

☐ Appears to be aware and oriented toward an activity and/or the environment

If NO, 🛑 *—this is not a teachable social moment*

Shared Space: Being in proximity to a skilled partner

☐ Close enough (five feet or less) to share focus and pleasure

---

Shared Focus: Both people paying attention to the same item or action

☐ Briefly pays attention to the same thing with a skilled partner

Shared Pleasure: Enjoying the same moment together

☐ Appears to experience pleasure with a skilled partner (e.g., smiles, glances, looks, laughs)

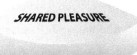

Social Engagement & the Steps to Being Social

LOWER 4

Regulated? Engaged?

| Yes | = move on |

| No | = go back |

Score:

0 = Not yet

1 = Beginning

2 = Practicing

3 = Got it

Being with a Skilled Partner (SP)

Proximity: Able to share the same space (not necessarily interacting or engaging in the same activity)

☐ Able to share the space (no more than five feet) without aggression or excess physical contact or vocalizations for at least five minutes

---

Parallel: Being with someone and using the same materials (though not necessarily for the same purpose)

☐ Tolerates skilled partner (SP) using the same materials within five feet

☐ Indicates by vocalization, gesture, or glance that an SP is using the same material or engaging in the same activity

☐ Indicates pleasure by smiling or other changes in expression

☐ Attends (e.g., looks at action or person) briefly to what the SP is doing

---

Joint Attention: Following, initiating, and visually attending to the same object or activity

☐ Attends to the same object or activity for at least three seconds

☐ Follows SP's direction to attend to an object of the learner's interest

☐ Initiates attention to an object of the learner's interest

☐ Alternates visual attention between object of interest and the SP

Reciprocal Exchange: Back-and-forth interaction

☐ Orients body/attends to the SP

☐ Maintains a brief shared focus with the SP

☐ Imitates a sound or action

☐ Takes an offered object

☐ Gives an object and/or directs a sound or action to the SP

☐ Waits with expectation (maintains body orientation) for a response

☐ Engages in a back-and-forth interaction for more than one exchange

MIDDLE 4

Regulated? Engaged?

Yes	= move on

No	= go back

Score:

0 = Not yet
1 = Beginning
2 = Practicing
3 = Got it

SP/TP   Being with a Skilled Partner (SP) or a Trained Peer (TP)

Reciprocal Exchange: Back-and-forth interaction

☐ Orients body/ attends to the SP/TP

☐ Maintains a brief shared focus with the SP/TP

☐ Imitates a sound or action

☐ Takes an offered object

☐ Gives an object and/or directs a sound or action to the SP/TP

☐ Waits with expectation (e.g., maintains body orientation) for a response

☐ Engages in back-and-forth interaction for more than one exchange

---

Give and Take of Conversation: Sending and receiving messages on the same topic

☐ Verbally or nonverbally responds to a message

☐ Intentionally directs a message (non-verbal or verbal)

☐ Matches facial expression to verbal communication or intended meaning

☐ Engages in back-and-forth conversation on a topic (at least three full exchanges)

Perspective Taking: Being aware that others have thoughts that are different from your own

☐ Indicates by a word or action an understanding that others can have different thoughts (e.g., questions, comments, or facial expressions related to someone else's feelings)

☐ Response or lack of response that indicates an acceptance that others can have different thoughts

☐ Identifies ways to figure out what others are thinking by reading nonverbal cues (e.g., tone, facial expressions, body language)

☐ Communicates that what others think has an impact on personal feelings

---

Reading the Social Scene: Noticing, attending to the relevant, and finding one's place

☐ Labels the social interactions within a given environment

☐ Attends to social situations for enough time to choose whether to join in

☐ Joins the social interaction

☐ Demonstrates methods to cope with nervousness and/or distress related to social performance (e.g., deep breaths, walks away, asks for help)

☐ Adjusts social communication based on social situation and partners

Social Engagement & the Steps to Being Social

Regulated? Engaged?

| Yes | = move on |
| No | = go back |

Score:

0 = Not yet
1 = Beginning
2 = Practicing
3 = Got it

SHARED SPACE
SHARED FOCUS
SELF REGULATION
SHARED PLEASURE

Reading the Social Scene: Noticing, attending to the relevant, and finding one's place

- [ ] Labels the social interactions within a given environment
- [ ] Attends to social situations for enough time to choose whether to join in
- [ ] Joins the social interaction
- [ ] Demonstrates methods to cope with nervousness and/or distress related to social performance (e.g., deep breaths, walks away, asks for help)
- [ ] Adjusts social communication based on social situation and partners

---

Group Cooperation: Having brain and body in the group, staying on topic and participating, and becoming aware of the need to be flexible with ideas

- [ ] Expresses desire to be part of a group
- [ ] Physically stays with the group and in own personal space
- [ ] Agrees on a topic or activity (e.g., suggests, negotiates)
- [ ] Participates when a topic/activity is chosen by someone else
- [ ] Appropriately breaks from or ends the interaction
- [ ] Recognizes that personal behavior affects thoughts and feelings of others
- [ ] Identifies and repairs a social mistake
- [ ] Adjusts behavior based on thoughts and feelings of others to be a part of the group

---

Friendship: Noticing that someone has similarities to you, accepting their differences, and finding reinforcing ways to be together

- [ ] Finds out what he/she has in common with another person
- [ ] Accepts things that are not in common
- [ ] Accepts that people can have more than one friend
- [ ] Appropriate use of social media
- [ ] Makes a plan to be with a friend (e.g., time, place, activity)
- [ ] Spends time together in more than one setting

Growing Connections: Maintaining a relationship over time, distance, changing circumstances, and varying levels of intimacy

- [ ] States differences in the types of friendship (e.g., best friend, girlfriend)
- [ ] States what information is typically shared in different types of relationships
- [ ] Maintains relationships over time
- [ ] Sustains relationships across distance
- [ ] States differences in various levels of intimacy
- [ ] States his/her own role in social relationships and conflicts
- [ ] Makes safe choices based on level of intimacy

The STEPS Assessment Summary

Name: _____ Time Period: _____

Date: _____ Activities: _____

Setting: _____

Skill Set: FOUNDATION   LOWER 4   MIDDLE 4   UPPER 4

Target Objectives:

1. _____

2. _____

3. _____

4. _____

Score:

0 = Not yet
1 = Beginning
2 = Practicing
3 = Got it

Proximity

Parallel

Joint Attention

Reciprocal Exchange

Give and Take

Perspective Taking

Reading the Social Scene

Group Cooperation

Friendship

Growing Connections

SELF-REGULATION

SHARED SPACE

SHARED FOCUS

SHARED PLEASURE

Interpreting the Scores

Yes / No   0,1,2,3

Social situations are affected by variables that are beyond our control. Keep this in mind when determining where the individual is on the social steps at various times and in changing situations. Think of the steps as a task analysis of social development. This dynamic process varies by the day, the people, and the environment.

Scores can be used to:

- Direct the therapy/interaction at the steps with scores of 1 or 2.
- Provide information for appropriately grouping learners.
- Guide the development of meaningful objectives.
- Track progress.

Data:

The sub-skills are set up so that a simple "yes" or "no" (i.e., the person can or cannot demonstrate this skill) allows for data collection. The data should drive the treatment approach, inform the instruction, and keep facilitators accountable.

Summary Sheet:

The summary sheet can be used as a visual representation of current performance and progress.

Evidence-Based Practices

Linking to the Skill Sets of the Social Steps

FOUNDATION

- Task Analysis
- Reinforcement
- Prompting
- Antecedent-based Intervention
- Parent-implemented Intervention
- Visual Supports (boundaries)

LOWER 4 (All FOUNDATION strategies as appropriate)

- Naturalistic Interventions
  - Joint Attention Training
- Discrete Trial Teaching
- Visual Supports (e.g., schedules, visual cues)

MIDDLE 4 (All FOUNDATION & LOWER 4 strategies as appropriate)

- Social Skills Training
- Social Narratives
- Video Modeling
- Peer-mediated Instruction and Intervention

UPPER 4 (All identified strategies above as appropriate)

- Self-Management

CHAPTER

6

Putting It All Together

Using the STEPS Assessment to Make a Social Plan

The Social Assessment has allowed you to decide where to begin. Identifying the skill sets that are at the "beginning" (coded 1) and "being practiced" (coded 2) levels show where treatment should be directed. The Social Plan is a tool to guide the intervention. Used as a worksheet, it can help you organize the information you have learned through assessment to create learning objectives and realistic plans for moving forward. The following four cases provide examples of a completed STEPS Assessment and Summary, as well as the follow-up Social Plan. In our practice, the Social Plan helps to ensure that we are using strategies as part of a plan and with purpose, always mindful that our activities and materials are age-appropriate and that the development of the needed skills are taught explicitly on the exciting journey of "being social."

Social Plan

Name: _____ Age: _____

Setting: _____

What skill set are you addressing?   FOUNDATION   LOWER 4   MIDDLE 4   UPPER 4

Objective:

_____

_____

What evidence-based practices will be used?

_____

_____

What materials do you need?

_____

_____

Where will you teach the skill set?

_____

_____

When and how often will you teach the skill set?

_____

_____

How will you teach the skill set?

_____

_____

How will you know the learner is making progress toward the objective?

_____

_____

How will this skill be generalized?

_____

_____

FOUNDATION: Scenario and Social Plan Example

Colleen is a nine-year-old girl with a diagnosis of ASD. She lives at home with her mom and dog. She loves to bounce on the trampoline, play in the sprinkler, hear the noise when she drops things, and watch certain videos. Colleen likes food, especially crunchy and chewy sweets. She likes it when food is used as a reinforcer but will try to grab the entire bag of food if she sees it.

Colleen is nonverbal but uses some gestures inconsistently to communicate. She will request preferred foods by bringing her mother or teacher the bag or container or pulling an adult's arm. At school, she is working on the Picture Exchange Communication System (PECS) and the progress is steady but slow.

Colleen's classroom has three staff and five students with ASD. The day is fairly structured with the same routine except for the students' therapies. Colleen prefers to pace in a particular part of the room that has windows. She is able to join the group for circle time, snack, and table time for approximately seven minutes if she has an adult next to her and her visual toys. At this time, she does not participate in activities and appears to be engaged with one person at a time for brief moments.

ENGAGEMENT

ENGAGEMENT is the Foundation to All Social Skills.

Score: [Yes] or [No]

Being with a Skilled Partner (SP)

Self-Regulation: Calm + Alert = READY to Learn

Y Appears to be in control of body and emotions: Stays in designated space without aggression, yelling, or overt signs of distress

Y Appears to be aware and oriented toward an activity and/or the environment

If NO, 🛑 *—this is not a teachable social moment*

Shared Space: Being in proximity to a skilled partner

N Close enough (five feet or less) to share focus and pleasure

---

Shared Focus: Both people paying attention to the same item or action

N Briefly pays attention to the same thing with a skilled partner

---

Shared Pleasure: Enjoying the same moment together

N Appears to experience pleasure with a skilled partner (e.g., smiles, glances, looks, laughs)

The STEPS Assessment Summary

Name: _Colleen_   Time Accessed: _1 hour_

Date: _7/24/2015_   Activities: _circle, transition, table work_

Setting: _classroom_

Skill Set: (FOUNDATION) LOWER 4   MIDDLE 4   UPPER 4

Score:

0 = Not yet
1 = Beginning
2 = Practicing
3 = Got it

Target Objectives:

1. _self-regulation_
2. _shared space_
3. _shared focus_
4. _shared pleasure_

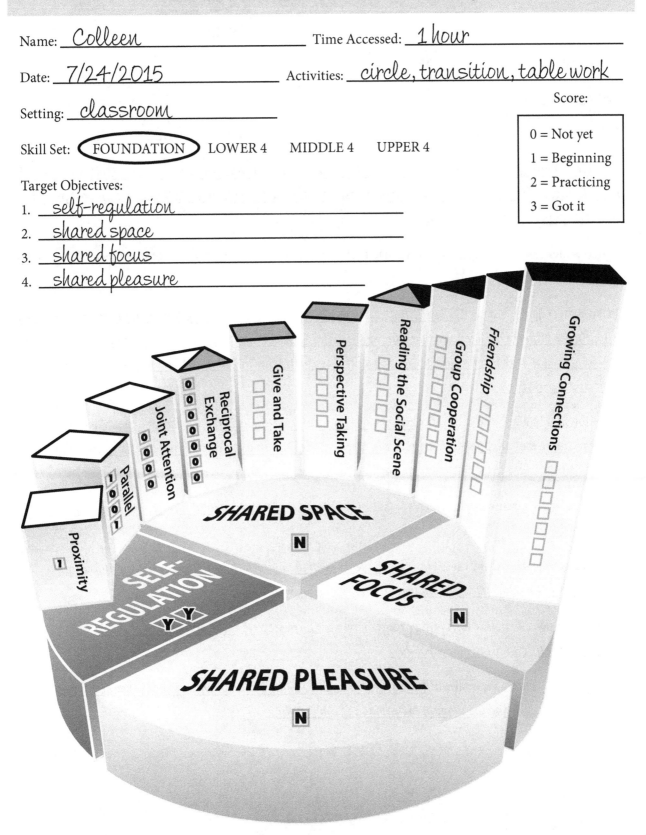

Social Plan

Name: *Colleen*   Age: *9*

Setting: *Classroom*

What skill set are you addressing?   *FOUNDATION*   LOWER 4   MIDDLE 4   UPPER 4

Objective: *During a structured activity, using highly desired items and given physical prompts, Colleen will actively engage (e.g., share space, focus, and pleasure) for at least two minutes with her teaching staff no less than four times during the school day.*

What evidence-based practices will be used? *Reinforcement, prompting, and visual supports/boundaries (environmental organization).*

What materials do you need? *Skittles (an edible that Colleen likes), bead stick/ball/water bottle with colored water (three or four visual objects that Colleen likes), large blocks and tin container with hole in it (structured put-in task that makes a sound), corner space in classroom with two physical boundaries (an environment with close proximity).*

Where will you teach the skill set? *Coat hooks, snack table, swing set area, classroom circle (determine four times in the school day that Colleen and the teaching staff are in close proximity with little distraction and where Colleen seems calm and ready to learn).*

When and how often will you teach the skill set? *Four times—beginning of day, snack, recess, and getting ready to go home.*

How will you teach the skill set? *Limit the space, control the materials, decrease the distractions around Colleen, and use fun and varied reinforcement.*

How will you know he/she is making progress toward the objective? *Colleen is able to engage for at least two minutes, four times during the school day.*

How will this skill be generalized? *Increase the frequency of the ENGAGEMENT opportunities, the duration of ENGAGEMENT, and the amount of people she engages with.*

LOWER 4: Scenario and Social Plan Example

Mark is a four-year-old boy with a diagnosis of ASD. He lives at home with his parents and two siblings. Mark loves any type of car and the pieces that make up cars. He likes to run, bounce, slide, and swing at the park. He likes to play with his siblings, usually in a chase game.

Mark loves routine and has significant difficulty with transitions and changes. Mark uses words to let someone know what he wants but if he is frustrated he screams. He uses a line-drawing picture schedule at school that is top down with a receptacle to match. Mark's classroom has two adults and six students with ASD. The days are structured with a similar routine, but the teacher uses the students' schedule to change up the routine to teach flexibility. Mark likes school and gives his teacher a hug each day.

Mark is interested in his peers. He watches them but does not understand how to play with them. He likes puzzles and fine motor games but needs them to be completed before he can move to the next activity. At circle time, Mark can wait for a peer to do something and he has been handing an object to one other person inconsistently.

Social Engagement & the Steps to Being Social

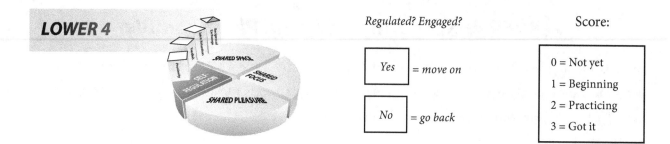

LOWER 4

Regulated? Engaged?

| Yes | = move on |

| No | = go back |

Score:

0 = Not yet
1 = Beginning
2 = Practicing
3 = Got it

Being with a Skilled Partner (SP)

Proximity: Able to share the same space (not necessarily interacting or engaging in the same activity)

3 Able to share the space (no more than five feet) without aggression or excess physical contact or vocalizations for at least five minutes

---

Parallel: Being with someone and using the same materials (though not necessarily for the same purpose)

3 Tolerates skilled partner (SP) using the same materials within five feet

3 Indicates by vocalization, gesture, or glance that an SP is using the same material or engaging in the same activity

2 Indicates pleasure by smiling or other changes in expression

3 Attends (e.g., looks at action or person) briefly to what the SP is doing

---

Joint Attention: Following, initiating, and visually attending to the same object or activity

3 Attends to the same object or activity for at least three seconds

3 Follows SP's direction to attend to an object of the learner's interest

2 Initiates attention to an object of the learner's interest

2 Alternates visual attention between object of interest and the SP

Reciprocal Exchange: Back-and-forth interaction

2 Orients body/attends to the SP

2 Maintains a brief shared focus with the SP

2 Imitates a sound or action

2 Takes an offered object

1 Gives an object and/or directs a sound or action to the SP

1 Waits with expectation (maintains body orientation) for a response

1 Engages in a back-and-forth interaction for more than one exchange

The STEPS Assessment Summary

Name: __Mark__   Time Accessed: __1 hour__

Date: __10/25/2015__   Activities: __recess, snack, free time__

Setting: __classroom__

Skill Set: FOUNDATION   (LOWER 4)   MIDDLE 4   UPPER 4

Score:
0 = Not yet
1 = Beginning
2 = Practicing
3 = Got it

Target Objectives:
1. __imitate others__
2. __give object and/or direct sound__
3. __wait with expectation__
4. __back and forth interaction__

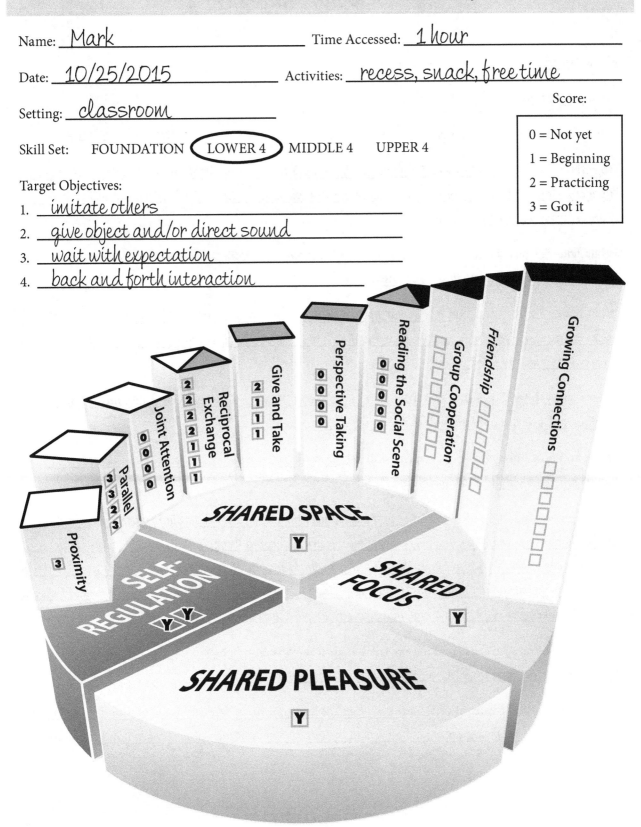

Social Plan

Name: _Mark_   Age: _4_

Setting: _Classroom_

What skill set are you addressing?   FOUNDATION   _LOWER 4_   MIDDLE 4   UPPER 4

Objective: _During a structured activity and given no more than two physical prompts (e.g., hand-over-hand support), Mark will actively participate in a reciprocal exchange with a peer by performing five object exchanges two times each school day._

What evidence-based practices will be used? _Reinforcement, prompting, visual supports (environmental organization), and naturalistic interventions._

What materials do you need? _A few matchbox cars (a motivator for Mark), puzzle of choice with 10 inset pieces (structured meaningful put-in task that Mark likes), space in classroom with decreased stimulation, three cube chairs and a table._

Where will you teach the skill set? _An area in a room with decreased distractions where three chairs can be lined up with puzzle board on table at the end of the line._

When and how often will you teach the skill set? _Two times a day: after snack time and before free choice. Picture schedule will indicate "social time."_

How will you teach the skill set? _Limit the space, control the materials, use familiar materials, and decrease the distractions around Mark and peers. Begin with Mark in the middle chair. Start puzzle pieces at one end of the line of chairs and pass it to Mark. With hand-over-hand support, have Mark pass it to the next child who puts it in the puzzle board on the table. Continue with all pieces and fade prompting. When puzzle is finished, show all students and give them a matchbox car to play with during Free Choice._

How will you know he/she is making progress toward the objective? _Mark is able to pass an object to a peer five times with no more than two prompts during a structured activity._

How will this skill be generalized? _Fade and then eliminate prompts. Increase frequency and number of exchanges. Increase opportunities to pass objects to include snack and lunch time. Talk to parents about doing this at home._

MIDDLE 4: Scenario and Social Plan Example

Liam is an 11-year-old boy who is in the process of diagnostic testing to consider the possibility that he has ASD. He lives at home with his parents, grandmother, and sister. Liam is very interested in specific airline companies, reading, computers, national parks, and video games. He likes to hang out at home in his room, travel with his family, and read facts about the national parks. Liam likes routine and sameness.

Liam is verbal and enjoys conversation, especially with adults. He likes to talk about his interests, often very loudly. Liam is in a general education fourth grade at an elementary school and the staff appreciates his kind personality. Although he wants to be included in peer social interactions, he is typically on the outside of social situations because he sometimes gets too close to others, dominates the conversation, and does not always understand what is going on around him. Liam is having difficulty connecting and making friends. Social situations happen in class, books, and recess that are often unclear to Liam and he frequently appears confused.

Liam likes to laugh and joke with peers but typically does not understand the jokes. He is just beginning to understand others' perspectives. Liam participates in an OT sensory/social group one time per week and his teacher receives OT consultation one time per week. Liam has made significant gains each year in therapy but continues to have difficulty understanding his social world at school.

Social Engagement & the Steps to Being Social

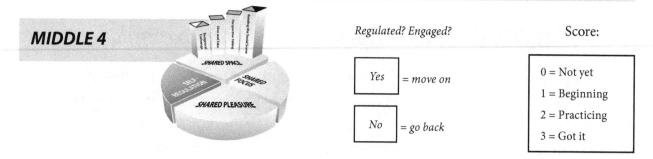

MIDDLE 4

Regulated? Engaged?

| Yes | = move on |

| No | = go back |

Score:

0 = Not yet

1 = Beginning

2 = Practicing

3 = Got it

SP/TP   Being with a Skilled Partner (SP) or a Trained Peer (TP)

Reciprocal Exchange: Back-and-forth interaction

3 Orients body/ attends to the SP/TP

3 Maintains a brief shared focus with the SP/TP

3 Imitates a sound or action

3 Takes an offered object

3 Gives an object and/or directs a sound or action to the SP/TP

3 Waits with expectation (e.g., maintains body orientation) for a response

3 Engages in back-and-forth interaction for more than one exchange

---

Give and Take of Conversation: Sending and receiving messages on the same topic

3 Verbally or nonverbally responds to a message

3 Intentionally directs a message (non-verbal or verbal)

2 Matches facial expression to verbal communication or intended meaning

2 Engages in back-and-forth conversation on a topic (at least three full exchanges)

Perspective Taking: Being aware that others have thoughts that are different from your own

2 Indicates by a word or action an understanding that others can have different thoughts (e.g., questions, comments, or facial expressions related to someone else's feelings)

1 Response or lack of response that indicates an acceptance that others can have different thoughts

2 Identifies ways to figure out what others are thinking by reading nonverbal cues (e.g., tone, facial expressions, body language)

1 Communicates that what others think has an impact on personal feelings

---

Reading the Social Scene: Noticing, attending to the relevant, and finding one's place

2 Labels the social interactions within a given environment

1 Attends to social situations for enough time to choose whether to join in

1 Joins the social interaction

0 Demonstrates methods to cope with nervousness and/or distress related to social performance (e.g., deep breaths, walks away, asks for help)

0 Adjusts social communication based on social situation and partners

---

The STEPS Assessment Summary

Name: Liam   Time Accessed: 45 minutes

Date: 11/15/2015   Activities: morning routine, math

Setting: classroom

Score:

Skill Set: FOUNDATION   LOWER 4   (MIDDLE 4)   UPPER 4

Score:
0 = Not yet
1 = Beginning
2 = Practicing
3 = Got it

Target Objectives:
1. match facial expressions
2. back and forth conversation 3 times
3. identify ways to figure out others' thinking
4. accept others' different thoughts

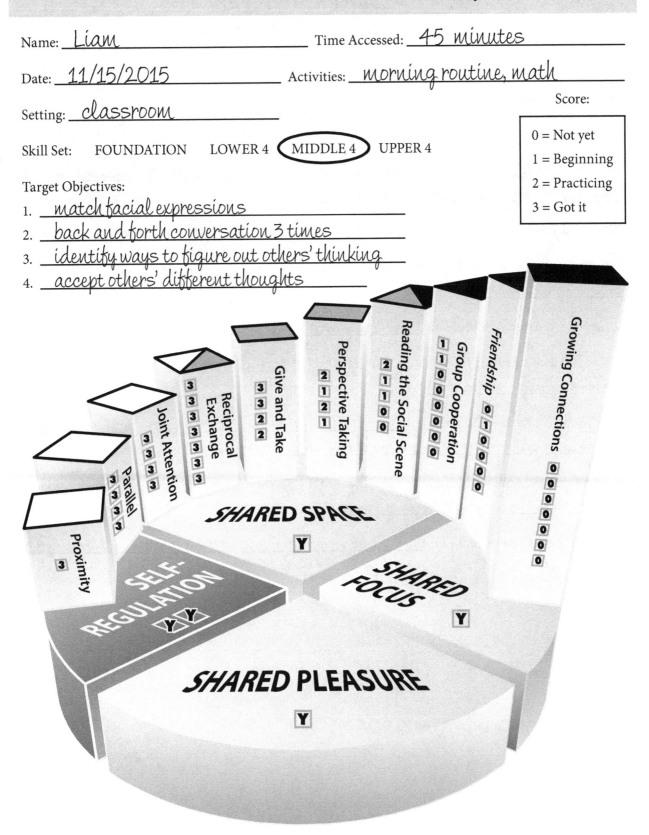

Social Plan

Name: *Liam*   Age: *11*

Setting: *Classroom*

What skill set are you addressing?   FOUNDATION   LOWER 4   *MIDDLE 4*   UPPER 4

Objective: *During a structured activity at the carpet area and given a visual prompt (volume scale), Liam will use appropriate voice volume when participating in group discussion.*

What evidence-based practices will be used? *Visual Supports, Social Skills Training, and Social Narratives.*

What materials do you need? *Visual cue of a volume scale with movable pieces, The Incredible 5-Point Scale by Kari Dunn Buron (2012).*

Where will you teach the skill set? *Carpet area activity.*

When and how often will you teach the skill set? *This will be practiced with the class at carpet time in the mornings three times per week.*

How will you teach the skill set? *Use a social narrative that includes vocabulary previously learned through therapy and a specific reward for lowering his volume during this time period.*

How will you know he/she is making progress toward the objective? *Liam will decrease his volume while at carpet time when presented with the visual prompt.*

How will this skill be generalized? *Liam will use appropriate volume with reduced prompting in a variety of settings.*

UPPER 4: Scenario and Social Plan Example

Gary is a 14-year-old boy with a diagnosis of ASD. He lives at home with his parents and grandparents. Gary loves *Star Trek*, reading, computers, and video games. He likes to hang out at home in his room, visit stores with video games, and play on his phone. Gary likes routine and sameness.

Gary is verbal and enjoys conversation if he is leading it and if it is about an interesting topic such as *Star Trek*. He is interested in and motivated by his peers, but peers report that he talks at them and not to them.

Gary attends his neighborhood middle school in all general education classes. He has trouble with organization and his writing is slow and messy. Gary has recently been referred to the counselor and social worker because he has almost gotten into three fights during lunch. It seems that Gary is being picked on because of his hygiene and grooming. Gary does not have a hygiene routine and typically forgets to brush his hair and teeth. At school, Gary hangs out with a couple of kids but he has never had anyone over to his house and he typically does his group projects alone.

Social Engagement & the Steps to Being Social

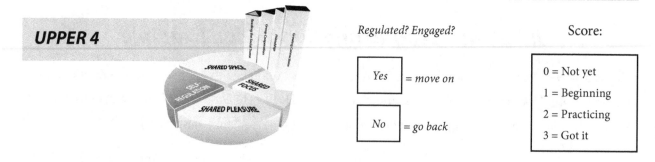

UPPER 4

Regulated? Engaged?

| Yes | = move on |
| No | = go back |

Score:

0 = Not yet
1 = Beginning
2 = Practicing
3 = Got it

Reading the Social Scene: Noticing, attending to the relevant, and finding one's place
3 Labels the social interactions within a given environment
3 Attends to social situations for enough time to choose whether to join in
2 Joins the social interaction
3 Demonstrates methods to cope with nervousness and/or distress related to social performance (e.g., deep breaths, walks away, asks for help)
3 Adjusts social communication based on social situation and partners

---

Group Cooperation: Having brain and body in the group, staying on topic and participating, and becoming aware of the need to be flexible with ideas
3 Expresses desire to be part of a group
3 Physically stays with the group and in own personal space
2 Agrees on a topic or activity (e.g., suggests, negotiates)
2 Participates when a topic/activity is chosen by someone else
1 Appropriately breaks from or ends the interaction
2 Recognizes that personal behavior affects thoughts and feelings of others
1 Identifies and repairs a social mistake
2 Adjusts behavior based on thoughts and feelings of others to be a part of the group

---

Friendship: Noticing that someone has similarities to you, accepting their differences, and finding reinforcing ways to be together
3 Finds out what he/she has in common with another person
2 Accepts things that are not in common
3 Accepts that people can have more than one friend
2 Appropriate use of social media
1 Makes a plan to be with a friend (e.g., time, place, activity)
1 Spends time together in more than one setting

Growing Connections: Maintaining a relationship over time, distance, changing circumstances, and varying levels of intimacy
1 States differences in the types of friendship (e.g., best friend, girlfriend)
1 States what information is typically shared in different types of relationships
2 Maintains relationships over time
0 Sustains relationships across distance
0 States differences in various levels of intimacy
0 States his/her own role in social relationships and conflicts
N/A Makes safe choices based on level of intimacy

The STEPS Assessment Summary

Name: *Gary* Time Accessed: *45 minutes*

Date: *9/3/2015* Activities: *game, discussion*

Setting: *social work setting*

Score:

Skill Set: FOUNDATION LOWER 4 MIDDLE 4 (UPPER 4)

Score:
0 = Not yet
1 = Beginning
2 = Practicing
3 = Got it

Target Objectives:

1. *hygiene*
2. *recognize own behavior impacts others*
3. *adjust behavior based on others' thoughts*
4. *negotiate*

Social Plan

Name: *Gary*   Age: *14*

Setting: *Social Work Session*

What skill set are you addressing?   FOUNDATION   LOWER 4   MIDDLE 4   *UPPER 4*

Objective: *At home each morning, given a verbal prompt from parents to watch a video model from his phone, Gary will brush his teeth and hair and place a checkmark on the provided self-management chart for five consecutive days.*

What evidence-based practices will be used? *Reinforcement, self-management, visual supports, and video model.*

What materials do you need? *Written hair and teeth routine, peer-acted video model, phone with video,* Star Trek *magazines, and recording chart.*

Where will you teach the skill set? *Social work session (develop and review hair and teeth routine and create and review self-management chart) one time per week to be used in the morning while in the bathroom at home.*

When and how often will you teach the skill set? *One time per week in social work session, and one time per day in the morning.*

How will you teach the skill set? *During a social work session, Gary will be introduced to a video model, "When you look messy, people mess with you." This video will be stored in Gary's phone. In the morning, Gary's parents will prompt him to watch the video after breakfast. Once teeth and hair are brushed, Gary will place a checkmark on the chart provided by the social worker. When Gary has five checkmarks, he earns a* Star Trek *magazine.*

How will you know he/she is making progress toward the objective? *Gary will get five checkmarks and receive the reinforcer.*

How will this skill be generalized? *Parent reminder is faded and replaced by beep on phone. Teeth and hair brushing are added to night routine, hair brushing added when getting ready to go out.*

Other Uses of Social Engagement & the Steps to Being Social

Our love for people with ASD is immense and as we have worked and re-worked the development of this model, the majority of our knowledge has been gained from learners with ASD in a therapy or educational setting. However, colleagues working in different settings with social learners who may or may not have ASD have taught us that this model can help them too.

Students with a mental health diagnosis:

Colleen Butcher, PhD, Psychology Postdoctoral Fellow, Division of Developmental and Behavioral Pediatrics at the Medical University of South Carolina

I am currently completing my PhD in school psychology. My area of research is on the definition and assessment of social skills. In furthering that research, I have conducted extensive literature reviews across multiple disciplines to answer questions such as, "What are social skills?" and "How are we measuring them?" I found that many fields have determined a few behaviors that are described as social skills, but that we do not have agreement across disciplines. What is lacking in the literature is a true, comprehensive model of what behaviors are required for a person to be socially successful. The Steps model offers a much more complete picture of the variety and developmental progression of skills necessary for social interaction and the creation of social relationships.

In my clinical work, I do assessment and therapy with children diagnosed with a range of mental health conditions, including mood disorders, trauma history, attention-deficit/hyperactivity disorder (ADHD), and neurodevelopmental disabilities. The Steps model is a very useful framework to first evaluate a child's strengths and weaknesses and then to conceptualize specific areas to target in treatment. A variety of mental health conditions can have a negative impact on a child's social functioning. For example, mood disorders, such as depression or anxiety, can lead to difficulties with being able to initiate interactions or develop relationships. Children with ADHD may have trouble picking up on relevant information in a social setting or staying on topic. In my own work, some of the elements of the steps that I have found particularly useful include self-regulation, perspective taking, reading the social scene, and group cooperation. However, other steps can also be important for children with diverse mental health needs. By identifying specific skills that provide the foundation for successful social functioning, I can determine measurable goals and specific strategies for intervention.

Neuro-typical peers and summer camp staff

Lauriann King, MFA Senior Program Specialist, UNM CDD Autism Program

It is intrinsic in human nature to seek engagement with others. In my experience, as a parent and professional in the autism field, individuals with autism are not the exception. They want to interact, but might have challenges in *how* to engage with others. Furthermore, the ability to engage with others creates more social learning opportunities and increases overall quality of life. We have used the foundation of **ENGAGEMENT** at Camp Rising Sun, a camp for children with autism and their peers. We teach: Being **READY**, shared space, shared focus, and shared pleasure to our peers and Counselors in Training (CITs). This is a natural and highly motivating way of increasing interaction between our typically developing peers and our campers with ASD in the camp setting. We also integrate, practice, and reinforce engagement throughout our camp session. As a result, campers with autism engage with their typically developing peers and the outcome is magical!

Family members of individuals with Fetal Alcohol Syndrome Disorder

Karen Wright MS, parent of a teen with Fetal Alcohol Syndrome Disorder

I am the mother of a 16-year-old young man with Fetal Alcohol Syndrome Disorder (FASD). This model has been helpful by providing a guide to support my son and his support team with an understanding of social development and the steps that are needed to being social in this complex world. Oftentimes, I and the people educating my son make assumptions about his social executive functioning skills. We assume he has naturally learned certain social nuances because of his many life experiences. I have found over and over again that it is important to teach these steps systematically in order for my son to make positive social choices in the world. This model provides wonderful guidance of what is needed in the world for even those who appear to be capable in many areas, but foundational social knowledge is missing. I have used the Steps model in supporting my son at school, in sports, in learning about friendships and relationships, and in learning how to be a positive member of a group. It has been invaluable.

Early interventionist and the families they serve

Kim Willard, PT, Early Interventionist, Gallup and Albuquerque, New Mexico

As a physical therapist working in the field of early intervention, I work with many children that have been exposed to trauma, whether it's from trauma of neglect in a chaotic household or the trauma of a noisy and brightly lit neonatal intensive care unit. Many of the infants and toddlers that I work with have fragile nervous systems that make learning more challenging. Following my introduction to *Social Engagement & the Steps to Being Social*, I began to look more carefully at states of arousal and the connections between states and the ability for social interaction and engagement. I found myself looking not only at the state of the child, but also the state of the parent in terms of everyone being present, being in an optimal place for learning. Talking to parents of very young children about getting the nervous system regulated before learning any skill and including social skills makes sense. It is a great introduction to some of the other tools that I might use in my work with a family such as, infant massage or specific ways of holding or positioning. Looking at motor development through the lens of ENGAGEMENT is now a critical part of the work I do.

The University of New Mexico's Masters of OT program

Heidi Sanders, MA, OTR/L - Faculty member with the University of New Mexico
Occupational Therapy Program

In the UNM Occupational Therapy Program, our students have a course that requires a semester-long fieldwork in a community mental health setting. Students are often asked to provide "social skills training," to individuals or groups, while at their fieldwork site. The term *social skills* encompasses a broad array of skills, and it is often overwhelming for students in this situation. "The Steps to Being Social" model provides a systematic breakdown of essential skills, allowing the students to assess baseline levels and organize individuals into similar groups for effective intervention. "The Steps to Being Social" also provides a starting point for intervention, as well as a developmental progression for goal writing and grading of intervention. In addition, the students appreciate the link to evidence-based practices provided for each level.

Teens with ASD and their family members

Jayme Swalby, MS, Special Education Teacher and parent of a teen with ASD

I have been traveling this journey with my son, Jeff, for 19 years, and today I have freedoms that I never thought possible several years ago. I like to believe that it is because of Jeff's determination and hard work combined with incredible people to support us that we have stumbled our way along this path to find a system that works. At home, I use *The Steps to Being Social* just about every day as a social development guide and reference. With Jeff's recent transition to college, he is facing new and unexpected social challenges, and I am working tirelessly to support while not intruding on his independence. Using the Steps model as my guide, I am able to identify what skills need to be taught or re-taught and create a plan for how to appropriately help Jeff generalize those skills. I find a sense of peace knowing that I have a strategy to use that helps keep me focused in a way that is simple, visual, and accessible.

The "Heart Start Model" incorporated the foundation of ENGAGEMENT in its early intervention model for children with high-risk FASD

Wendy Kalberg, MA, LED Principal Investigator/Clinical Research Associate

The Foundation of ENGAGEMENT is incorporated into The Heart Start Early Intervention Model (Kalberg, Laurel, & Taylor, 2013) that is being used in the Western Cape region of South Africa for the early intervention initiative. The philosophical underpinning of the model is that positive developmental outcomes of the child occur in the context of meaningful relationships and the social/emotional well-being of the child and the family.

Because the central tenant of this work is to promote trusting relationships between children and their caregivers, we have incorporated the Foundation of **ENGAGEMENT** within our model. This useful tool has resonated well with the families and intervention staff with whom we are working. Using the Foundation of **ENGAGEMENT** language of shared space, shared focus, and shared pleasure and the need for the child to be calm and alert and ready (C+A=R) to engage has been extremely helpful to our process.

School therapists serving children with a variety of abilities

Kristen Red-Horse MOT/L, School Occupational Therapist

As a pediatric occupational therapist working with children, parents/caregivers, and educators, I support children with a wide range of unique developmental challenges ages 1 to 18 years old. I have been fortunate to have many amazing teachers including children who have hearing loss, ADD, ADHD, sensory processing disorder, cerebral palsy, Down syndrome, autism spectrum disorder, emotional and behavioral challenges, language and communication delays, and more. I work side-by-side with therapists, teachers, and parents to problem solve children's learning concerns and have found the Foundation of **ENGAGEMENT** to be a simple, clear tool for explaining goals as part of a collaborative relationship. For example, drawing the four components of **ENGAGEMENT** using a dry erase board, I have explained to a teacher about the magic social learning moment she just created for a student. It was a quick, clear way to illustrate how, by offering an activity that helped the student regulate, he was able to share the space, focus, and pleasure. This model lends itself to assessment, planning, and reflection in preschool, school, community, and home environments.

Developmental teams serving children in foster care

Heidi Sanders, MA, OTR/L—Working in collaboration with La Familia Treatment Foster Care

Children in treatment foster care have often missed early opportunities for developing positive relationships. As an occupational therapist working with children in treatment foster care, the goals include supporting co-regulation between the parent and child, helping the child learn skills for self-regulation, helping the child form attachment to a parental figure, and supporting sensory, motor, cognitive, and social emotional development. Social Engagement & the Steps to Being Social is an effective tool toward reaching many of these goals. The foundation of **ENGAGEMENT** is a wonderful graphic to share with parents and supporting staff. It describes the components for creating opportunities for attachment and bonding during play, as well as caregiving activities. For these children, the components of **ENGAGEMENT** must also be in place for a child to begin co-regulation with a parent. Once this is established, the child can begin to learn skills for his or her own self-regulation. Occupational therapists, as well as other professionals working with children with a history of trauma or neglect, can utilize this model to guide attachment-focused interventions.

Individuals in the juvenile justice system

Hannah Bloom, MOTR/L, Occupational Therapy Consultant

As an occupational therapist working in confinement facilities of the juvenile justice system in New Mexico, I have found the use of the *Social Engagement & the Steps to Being Social* assessment extremely beneficial as a framework for intervention planning and assessment of prosocial behaviors. The ultimate goal of most of my clients is to return to their communities, find meaningful occupation, and meaningful roles as citizens. In order to meet these goals, a client needs to be able to regulate his or her nervous and sensory systems.

In addition, a number of the higher level social skills outlined in the Steps to Being Social are challenging for the majority of my clients. It has allowed me to use the higher level cognitive skills (**UPPER 4** sub-skills) to develop goals, while also attending to the sensory needs to determine social readiness. I have found this model lays out the necessary steps for an individual to be successful in friendship, relationship, and community involvement.

Summary

Becoming engaged in social interaction and beginning to climb the "steps to being social" is a dynamic and complex process. We hope that this model provides a sequence of learning in a visual framework that is easy to understand and put into practice. It is meant to support the assessment of social skills and guide in the development of interventions. It also takes into consideration the need to teach skills in a variety of settings and with a variety of people and to provide many opportunities to practice. We have learned that teaching social skills requires flexibility and creativity as we traverse the day-to-day complexities of social interaction. Conceptualized at times as stairs, an escalator, or an elevator, the model encourages learners to develop the skills that will enhance their range of life choices and ultimately lead to a better quality of life. By writing this book, we hope we lessened the mystery of teaching social skills and honored both the art and the science of the work. We thank you for engaging with us in thinking about the wonder of "being social."

APPENDICES

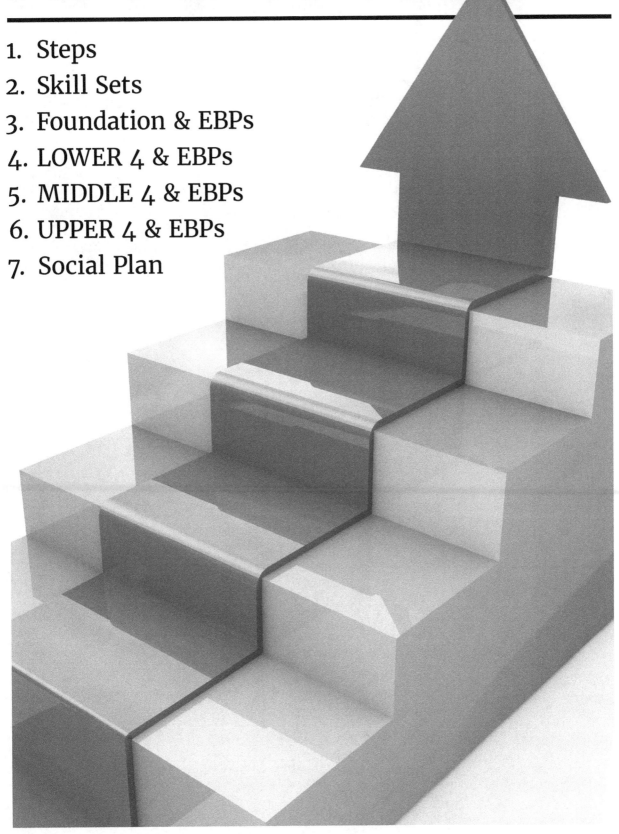

Social Engagement & the Steps to Being Social

(Access this page at http://fhautism.com/socialengagement.html)

Proximity
Parallel
Joint Attention
Reciprocal Exchange
Give and Take
Perspective Taking
Reading the Social Scene
Group Cooperation
Friendship
Growing Connections

SHARED SPACE
SHARED FOCUS
SELF-REGULATION
SHARED PLEASURE

© 2016 Taylor, Laurel

The Four Skill Sets

(Access this page at http://fhautism.com/socialengagement.html)

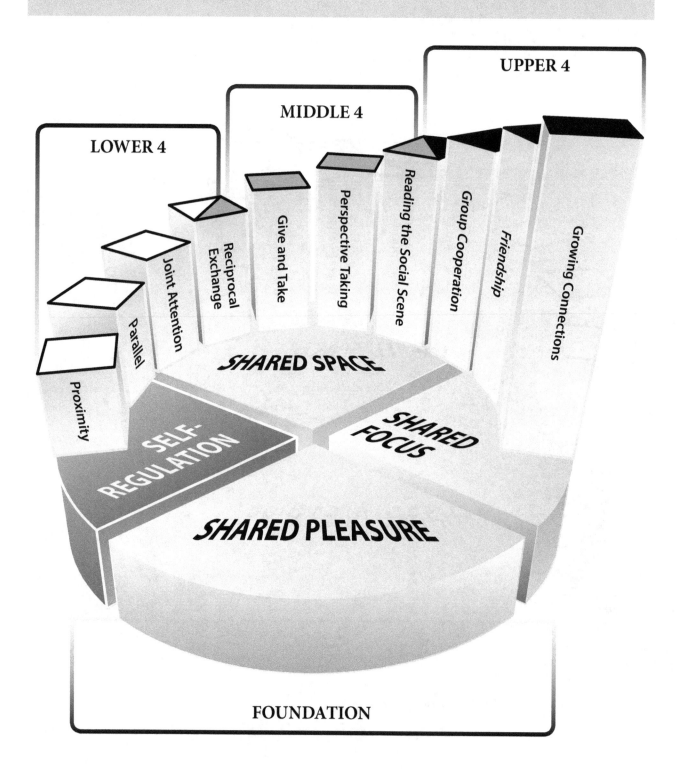

UPPER 4

MIDDLE 4

LOWER 4

Proximity

Parallel

Joint Attention

Reciprocal Exchange

Give and Take

Perspective Taking

Reading the Social Scene

Group Cooperation

Friendship

Growing Connections

SHARED SPACE

SELF-REGULATION

SHARED FOCUS

SHARED PLEASURE

FOUNDATION

FOUNDATION *(Access this page at http://fhautism.com/socialengagement.html)*

ENGAGEMENT is the Foundation for the Steps to Being Social.

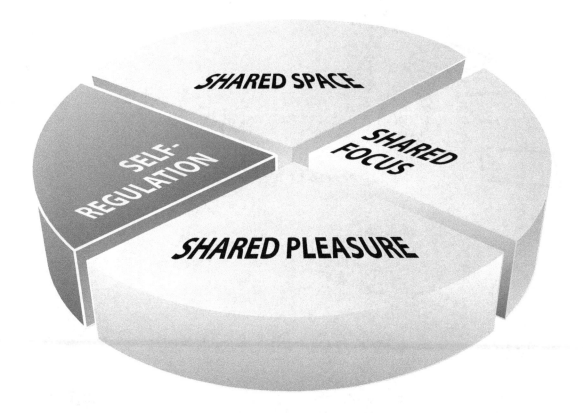

Evidence-Based Practices:

- Task Analysis
- Parent-implemented Interventions
- Prompting
- Reinforcement
- Antecedent-based Interventions
- Visual Supports (boundaries)

© 2016 Taylor, Laurel

LOWER 4 Steps to Being Social

(Access this page at http://fhautism.com/ socialengagement.html)

LOWER 4—a time of learning to be together with a social partner and beginning to understand, and indeed be motivated by, back-and-forth interaction.

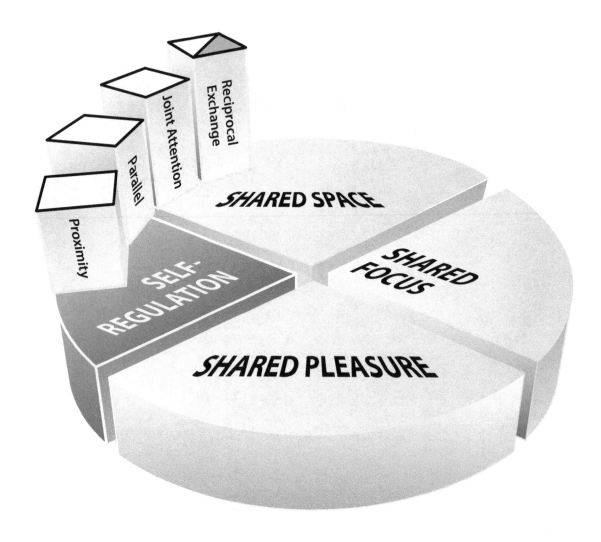

Evidence-Based Practices:

- Strategies from **FOUNDATION**
- Visual Supports
- Discrete Trial Teaching
- Naturalistic Interventions
  - Joint Attention Training

© 2016 Taylor, Laurel

MIDDLE 4 Steps to Being Social

(Access this page at http://fhautism.com/ socialengagement.html)

MIDDLE 4—a time to learn to use directed communication and understand that others have different ideas and that there is indeed much social activity happening all around.

Evidence-Based Practices:

- Strategies from *FOUNDATION* and *LOWER 4*
- Social Skills Training
- Social Narratives
- Video Modeling
- Peer-mediated Instruction and Intervention

© 2016 Taylor, Laurel

UPPER 4 Steps to Being Social

(Access this page at http://fhautism.com/ socialengagement.html)

UPPER 4—involve the logical final steps to long-lasting meaningful relationships that are the work of every person's lifetime.

Evidence-Based Practices:

- Strategies from *FOUNDATION*, *LOWER 4*, and *MIDDLE 4*
- Self-Management

Social Plan

(Access this page at http://fhautism.com/socialengagement.html)

Name: _____ Age: _____

Setting: _____

What skill set are you addressing?   FOUNDATION   LOWER 4   MIDDLE 4   UPPER 4

Objective:

_____

_____

What evidence-based practices will be used?

_____

_____

What materials do you need?

_____

_____

Where will you teach the skill set?

_____

_____

When and how often will you teach the skill set?

_____

_____

How will you teach the skill set?

_____

_____

How will you know the learner is making progress toward the objective?

_____

_____

How will this skill be generalized?

_____

_____

Thank you

The development of this model and the process of writing this book have been a journey, a bit like ascending a large staircase with friends, colleagues, and children with ASD and their families. Some of these incredible people have been walking the staircase for our entire journey and some have jumped on for a short time. Our hope is that every person understands that he or she has made a contribution and we thank you!

Social Engagement & the Steps to Being Social would not be as clearly defined or objective without the incredible contribution of Maryann Trott, MA, BCBA. She patiently discussed, read, re-read, and helped revise the sub-steps and reviewed the entire manuscript in detail in the hope that others can use this model successfully. In addition, we appreciate and honor the support and contributions of the University of New Mexico Center for Development and Disability Autism and Other Developmental Disabilities Programs toward the development and improvement of this work. Tremendous thanks to Brenda Smith Myles for her enthusiasm and encouragement and for starting us on the path to writing.

Our huge appreciation to friends and colleagues who have contributed so generously to the entire process: Wendy Kalberg, Kim Willard, Hannah Bloom, Heidi Sanders, Pat Osbourn, Karen Wright, Lauriann King, and Pat Burtner. Without you, our direction and confidence could have waned. We appreciate you moving us forward.

We also thank all those who have stepped into this journey at one time or another: Sylvia Acosta, Lori Bieri, Mary Boehm, Paul Brouse, Courtney Burnette, Colleen Butcher, Mikki Chavez, Cheryl Cotter, Rita Crozier, Slava Dovbnya, Kathryn Faturos, Logan Gillespie, Stephanie Graner, Mark Hartman, Mary Jimerson, Lisa Kalberg, Cynthia King, Mary Mandeville-Chase, Paul Martinez, Tanya Morozova, Kristen Red-Horse, Sylvia Sarmiento, Debra Sugar, Jayme Swalby, Chris Vining, Carla Cay Williams, Maia Wynn, Ian Zachary, the early intervention cohort at Stellenbosh University, South Africa, the Russian school and camp cohorts, the Nicaraguan early intervention and school teams, and the many OT students who have participated in "Theraplay." Your excitement about our ideas has been infectious. Special thanks to Linda Lombardino for her long-ago mentorship around the magic of engagement.

To the families of children we have worked with to climb the social steps, including through "Theraplay," the CDD Autism Programs, and Camp Rising Sun—thank you for sharing your children, your time, and your trust. Your courage and belief in all people "being social" has been inspiring. And to the children and adults with ASD with whom we have been given the opportunity to share time, may you know deep inside that you are the finest teachers out there, THANK YOU.

Finally to our families: Pat, Dorothy, Cal, Hallie, Azucena, Alejandro, Jack, Keenan, and Shane, who not only had to walk the staircase alongside us, but at times, repair the staircase, clean the staircase, paint the staircase… We thank you for your love and support and for staying excited with us about this journey.

REFERENCES

REFERENCES

BOOKS

American Psychiatric Association. (2013). *Diagnostic and Statistical Manual of Mental Disorders: DSM-5.* Washington, DC

Aspy R. & Grossman B. (2007). *The Ziggurat Model: A Framework for Designing Comprehensive Interventions for Individuals with High-functioning Autism and Asperger Syndrome.* Lenexa, KS: AAPC Publishing.

Atwood, T. & Wing, L. (1998). *Asperger's Syndrome: A Guide for Parents and Professionals.* Philadelphia, PA: Jessica Kingsley Publishers.

Ayers, A. J. (1979), *Sensory Integration and the Child.* Los Angeles, CA: Western Psychological Services.

Bellini, S. (2006). *Building Social Relationships: A Systematic Approach to Teaching Social Interaction Skills to Children and Adolescents with Autism Spectrum Disorders and other Social Difficulties.* Lenexa, KS: AAPC Publishing.

Baron-Cohen, S. (1997). *Mindblindness: An Essay on Autism and Theory of Mind.* Cambridge, MA: MIT Press.

Baron-Cohen, S., Leslie, A. M., & Frith, U. (1985). Does the Autistic Child Have a "Theory of Mind"? *Cognition,* 21, 37-46.

Benton, M., Hollis, C., Mahler, K., & Womer, A. (2011). *Destination Friendship: Developing Social Skills for Individuals with Autism Spectrum Disorders or Other Social Challenges.* Shawnee Mission, KS: AAPC Publishing.

Beytien, A. (2011). *Autism Every Day.* Arlington, TX: Future Horizons.

Buron, K. D. & Curtis, M. (2012). *Incredible 5 Point Scale: The Significantly Improved and Expanded Second Edition; Assisting Students in Understanding Social Interactions and Controlling Their Emotional Responses.* Lenexa, KS: AAPC Publishing.

Endow, J. (2012). *Learning the Hidden Curriculum: The Odyssey of One Autistic Adult.* Shawnee Mission, KS: AAPC Publishing.

Endow, J., Mayfield, M. & Myles, B. S. (2012). *The Hidden Curriculum of Getting and Keeping a Job: Navigating the Social Landscape of Employment.* Lenexa, KS: AAPC Publishing.

Frost, L. & Bondy, A. (2002). *Picture Exchange Communication* (2nd Ed.). Newark, DE: Pyramid Educational Consultants.

Grandin, T. & Panek, R. (2014). *The Autistic Brain: Helping Different Kinds of Minds Succeed.* New York, NY: Houghton Mifflin Hardcourt Publishing.

Grandin, T. (2006). *Thinking in Pictures: My Life with Autism.* New York, NY: Random House.

Gray, C. (2000). *Writing Social Stories with Carol Gray: Accompanying Workbook to DVD.* Arlington, TX: Future Horizons, Inc.

Janzen, J. & Moore, D. (1998). *Understanding the Nature of Autism: A Practical Guide.* Alexandria: VA: Psychological Corp.

Koegel, R. L. & Koegel, L. K. (2006). *Pivotal Response Treatments for Autism: Communication, Social, & Academic Development.* Baltimore, MD: Paul H. Brookes Publishing Company.

Laurel, M. & Williams C. C. (2013). *Our Hearts' Desire: For Families Navigating the Journey of Sensory Processing Challenges.* North Charleston, SC: CreateSpace.

Margulies, N. & Maal, N. (2001). *Mapping Inner Space: Learning and Teaching Visual Mapping* (2nd ed.). Thousand Oaks, CA: Corwin Press.

McAfee, J. & Attwood, T. (2013). *Navigating the Social World: A Curriculum for Individuals with Asperger's Syndrome, High Functioning Autism and Related Disorders.* Arlington, TX: Future Horizons, Inc.

Mesibov, G. B., Shea, V., & Schopler, E. (2004). *The TEACCH Approach to Autism Spectrum Disorders.* New York City, NY: Springer Publishing.

Committee on Integrating the Science of Early Childhood Development and Board on Children, Youth and Families (2000). *From Neurons to Neighborhoods: The Science of Early Childhood Development.* Washington, DC: National Academies Press.

Mundy, P. & Burnette, C. (2005). Joint Attention and Neurodevelopmental Models of Autism. In Volkmar, F.R., R. Paul, A. Klin, & D. Cohen. *Handbook of Autism and Pervasive Developmental Disorders* (650-681). Hoboken, NJ: John Wiley & Sons.

Myles, B. S. & Southwick, J. (2005). *Asperger Syndrome and Difficult Moments: Practical Solutions for Tantrums, Rage and Meltdowns.* Lenexa, KS: AAPC Publishing.

Myles, B. S., Trautma, M. L., & Schelvan, R. L. (2013). *The Hidden Curriculum for Understanding Unstated Rules in Social Situations for Adolescents and Young Adults.* Lenexa, KS: AAPC Publishing.

National Research Council (2001). *Educating Children with Autism.* Washington, DC: National Academy Press.

REFERENCES

Oetter, P., Richter, E. W., & Frick, S. M. (1995). *M.O.R.E. Integrating the Mouth with Sensory and Postural Functions*. Hugo, MN: Professional Development Press.

Prizant, B. M., Wetherby, A. M., Rubin, E., Laurent, A. C., & Rydell, P. J. (2006) *The SCERTS Model: A Comprehensive Educational Approach for Children with Autism Spectrum Disorders*. Baltimore, MD: Paul Brookes.

Reaven, J., Blakeley-Smith, A., Nichols, S., & Hepburn, S. (2011). *Facing Your Fears: Group Therapy for Managing Anxiety in Children with High-Functioning Autism Spectrum Disorders*. Baltimore, MD: Paul H. Brookes Publishing Co.

Reichow, B., Doehring, P, Cicchetti, D. V., & Volkmar, F. R. (2011). *Evidenced Based Practices and Treatments for Children with Autism*. New York, NY: Springer.

Richter, E. W. & Oetter, P. (1990) Environmental matrices for sensory integrative treatment, S.C. Merrill (Ed). Environment: Implications for occupational therapy practice—a sensory integrative perspective. Rockville, MD: American Occupational Therapy Association, Inc.

Rogers, S. J. & Dawson, G. (2010). *Early Start Denver Model for Young Children with Autism: Promoting Language, Learning & ENGAGEMENT*. New York, NY: Guilford Press.

Sussman, F. (2012). *More Than Words*. Toronto, ON: Hanen Centre.

Thierfeld Brown, Wolf, Kind, & Bork (2012). *The Parent's Guide to College for Students on the Autism Spectrum*, Lenexa, KS: AAPC Publishing.

Ticani, M. & Bondy, A. (2015). *Autism Spectrum Disorders in Adolescents and Adults: Evidence-Based and Promising Interventions*. New York, NY: Guilford Press.

Trott, M. C., Laurel, M. K., & Windeck, S. L. (1993). *Sense Abilities: Understanding Sensory Integration*. Tucson, AZ: Therapy Skill Builders.

Williams M. S. & Shellenberger, S. (1996). *How Does Your Engine Run? A Leader's Guide to the Alert Program™ for Self Regulation*. Albuquerque, NM: TherapyWorks, Inc.

Winner, M. G. (2007). *Thinking About YOU Thinking About ME*, (2nd ed.). San Jose, CA: Think Social Publications, Inc.

Winner, M. G. (2009). *Politically Incorrect Look at Evidence-Based Practices and Teaching Social Skills: A Literature Review and Discussion*. San Jose, CA: Think Social Publications, Inc.

Winner, M. G. (2005). *Think Social! A Social Thinking Curriculum for School-Age Students.* San Jose, CA: Think Social Publications, Inc.

Winner, M. G. & Crooke, P. (2008). *You Are a Social Detective.* San Jose, CA: Think Social Publications, Inc.

PRESENTATIONS

Beytien, A. (April, 2016). "Mermaid Trouble: Navigating the Sea of Adolescence and Autism." Presentation at the University of New Mexico Autism Imagine Conference, Albuquerque, NM.

Boehm, M. (2016). "Evidence Based Practice for Autism Spectrum Disorder." University of New Mexico Center for Development and Disability Autism and Other Developmental Disabilities Programs. Retrieved from: cdd.unm.edu/autism/program

Fuhrmeister, S., Lozett, E., & Stapel-Wax, J. (November 2015). "Creating Sustainable Systems of Support for Young Children at Risk for ASD across Settings." Presentation at the American Speech Language and Hearing Association National Convention, Denver, CO.

Kalberg, W., Laurel, M., & Taylor, K. M. (2013, August). "The Heart Start Model for Early Intervention with Children with Fetal Alcohol Spectrum Disorder." Week-long course presented for the University of New Mexico Center for Alcoholism, Substance Abuse and Addictions, Robertson, South Africa.

Klin, A. (November 2014). Keynote presentation at the OCALICON, Columbus, Ohio.

Myles, B. S. (April, 2016). "The Hidden Curriculum of Keeping a Job." Presentation at the University of New Mexico Autism Imagine Conference, Albuquerque, NM.

Rydell, P. & Treharne, S. (November, 2015). "Six IEP Goals for Addressing Social Anxiety in ASD." Short course presented at the American Speech Language and Hearing Association National Convention, Denver, CO.

ARTICLES

Barnhill Outcomes in Adults with Asperger Syndrome, *Focus on Autism and Other Developmental Disabilities*, 22(2) (Summer 2007), 116-126.

Bellini, S., Peters, J. K., Benner, L., & Hopf, A. (2007). A meta-analysis of school-based social skills interventions for children with ASD. *Journal of Remedial and Special Education*, 28(3), 153-162.

Butcher, C. M. (2016). Examining the social validity of a dynamic assessment of social skills: Caregivers' perspectives on a measure of social skills for children with autism spectrum disorders (Unpublished doctoral dissertation). University of Florida, Gainesville, FL.

DeMatteo, F. J., Arter, P. S., Sworen-Parise, C., Fanciana, M., & Paulhamus, M. A. (2012). Social skills training for young adults with autism spectrum disorder: Overview and implications for practice. *National Teacher Education Journal*, 5(4).

Gillespie, L. G. & Seibel, N. L. (2006). Self-regulation: A cornerstone of early childhood development. *Young Children*, 61(4), 34-39.

Mesibov, G. G. & Shea, V. (2010). The TEACCH program in the era of evidence-based practice. *Journal of Autism and Developmental Disorders*, 40(5), 570-579.

Odom, S. Hume, K., Boyd, B., & Stabel A. (2012). Moving beyond the intensive behavior treatment versus eclectic dichotomy: Evidence-based and individualized programs for learners with ASD. *Behavior Modification*, 36(3), 270-297.

Schreibman, L., Dawson, G., Stahmer, A. C., Landa, R., Rogers, S. J., McGee, G. C., Kasari, C., Ingersoll, B., Kaiwer, A. P., Bruinsma, Y., McNerney, E., Wetherby, A., & Halladay, A. (2015). Naturalistic developmental behavioral interventions: Empirically validated treatments for autism spectrum disorder. *Journal of Autism and Developmental Disorders*, 10.1007/s10803-015-2407-8, 2412-2427.

Tomchek, S. D., Little, L. M., & Dunn, W. (2015). Sensory pattern contributions to developmental performance in children with autism spectrum disorder. *American Journal of Occupational Therapy*, 69(5), 1-10.

NPDC PRACTICES

AFIRM Team. (2015) Antecedent-based intervention. Chapel Hill, NC: National Professional Development Center on Autism Spectrum Disorders, FPG Child Development Center, University of North Carolina. Retrieved from http://afirm.fpg.unc.edu/antecedent-based-intervention

Bogin, J. (2008). Overview of discrete trial training. Sacramento, CA: National Professional Development Center on Autism Spectrum Disorders, M.I.N.D. Institute, University of California at Davis Medical School.

Collet-Klingenberg, L. (2009). Overview of social skills groups. Madison, WI: National Professional Development Center on Autism Spectrum Disorders, Waisman Center, University of Wisconsin.

Collet-Klingenberg, L. & Franzone, E. (2008). Overview of social narratives. Madison, WI: National Professional Development Center on Autism Spectrum Disorders, Waisman Center, University of Wisconsin.

Franzone, E. & Collet-Klingenberg, L. (2008). Overview of video modeling. Madison, WI: National Professional Development Center on Autism Spectrum Disorders, Waisman Center, University of Wisconsin.

Franzone, E. (2009). Overview of task analysis. Madison, WI: National Professional Development Center on Autism Spectrum Disorders, Waisman Center, University of Wisconsin.

Franzone, E. (2009). Overview of naturalistic intervention. Madison, WI: National Professional Development Center on Autism Spectrum Disorders, Waisman Center, University of Wisconsin.

Hendricks, D. R. (2009). Overview of parent-implemented intervention. Chapel Hill, NC: National Professional Development Center on Autism Spectrum Disorders, Frank Porter Graham Child Development Institute, University of North Carolina.

Hume, K. (2008). Overview of visual supports. Chapel Hill, NC: National Professional Development Center on Autism Spectrum Disorders, Frank Porter Graham Child Development Institute, University of North Carolina.

Neitzel, J. Overview of reinforcement. Chapel Hill, NC: National Professional Development Center on Autism Spectrum Disorders, Frank Porter Graham Child Development Institute, University of North Carolina.

Neitzel, J. & Wlery, M. (2009). Overview of prompting. Chapel Hill, NC: National Professional Development Center on Autism Spectrum Disorders, Frank Porter Graham Child Development Institute, University of North Carolina.

Neitzel, J. (2008). Overview of peer-mediated instruction and intervention for children and youth with autism spectrum disorders. Chapel Hill, NC: National Professional Development Center on Autism Spectrum Disorders, Frank Porter Graham Child Development Institute, University of North Carolina.

Neitzel, J. & Busick, M. (2009). Overview of self-management. Chapel Hill, NC: National Professional Development Center on Autism Spectrum Disorders, Frank Porter Graham Child Development Institute, University of North Carolina.

Neitzel, J. (2009). Overview of antecedent-based interventions. Chapel Hill, NC: National Professional Development Center on Autism Spectrum Disorders, Frank Porter Graham Child Development Institute, University of North Carolina.

About the Authors

Kathleen "Mo" Taylor, OTR/L is an occupational therapist with a 30-year history of working with children, adolescents and adults with Autism Spectrum Disorder (ASD). Mo works at the University of New Mexico Center for Development and Disability Autism and Other Developmental Disabilities Programs. She teaches and consults around evidence based practices for individuals with ASD. In addition, Mo has a private practice, Theraplay, where she provides therapy and consultation for people with ASD, Sensory Processing Disorder, and Behavioral Differences across the life span. Mo facilitates sensory/social groups and also consults within the community to help provide appropriate evidence based supports and accommodations for individuals with ASD in classroom, community and home settings. She has shared her experiences through trainings around New Mexico, nationally and internationally. Her career has been devoted to better "real life" outcomes for all individuals.

Marci Laurel, MA, CCC-SLP is a Speech-Language Pathologist with the University of New Mexico Center for Development and Disability Autism and Other Developmental Disabilities Programs. Marci has practiced in Albuquerque for the past 35 years providing direct services, consultation, training, and student supervision in public school, private practice, and university settings. She has lectured nationally and internationally on topics related to sensory processing and communication, family issues and Autism Spectrum Disorder. Marci is co-author of several related publications, most recently *Our Hearts' Desire: For Families Navigating the Journey of Sensory Processing Challenges*.

DID YOU LIKE THE BOOK?

Rate it and share your opinion.

amazon.com   **BARNES & NOBLE**
                        BOOKSELLERS
                        www.bn.com

Not what you expected? Tell us!

Most negative reviews occur when the book did not reach expectation. Did the description build any expectations that were not met? Let us know how we can do better.

Please drop us a line at *info@fhautism.com*.

Thank you so much for your support!

CPSIA information can be obtained
at www.ICGtesting.com
Printed in the USA
BVHW091928160120
569553BV00001B/3